Prisoner of Wars

In the series *Asian American History and Culture*, edited by Cathy Schlund-Vials, Shelley Sang-Hee Lee, and Rick Bonus. Founding editor, Sucheng Chan; editors emeriti, David Palumbo-Liu, Michael Omi, K. Scott Wong, and Linda Trinh Võ.

ALSO IN THIS SERIES:

Heidi Kim, *Illegal Immigrants/Model Minorities: The Cold War of Chinese American Narrative* (forthcoming)

Kavita Daiya, *Graphic Migrations: Precarity and Gender in India and the Diaspora* (forthcoming)

Timothy K. August, *The Refugee Aesthetic: Reimagining Southeast Asian America* (forthcoming)

L. Joyce Zapanta Mariano, *Giving Back: Filipino Diaspora and the Politics of Giving* (forthcoming)

Manan Desai, *The United States of India: Anticolonial Literature and Transnational Refraction*

Cathy J. Schlund-Vials, Guy Beauregard, and Hsiu-chuan Lee, eds., *The Subject(s) of Human Rights: Crises, Violations, and Asian/American Critique*

Malini Johar Schueller, *Campaigns of Knowledge: U.S. Pedagogies of Colonialism and Occupation in the Philippines and Japan*

Crystal Mun-hye Baik, *Reencounters: On the Korean War and Diasporic Memory Critique*

Michael Omi, Dana Y. Nakano, and Jeffrey T. Yamashita, eds., *Japanese American Millennials: Rethinking Generation, Community, and Diversity*

Masumi Izumi, *The Rise and Fall of America's Concentration Camp Law: Civil Liberties Debates from the Internment to McCarthyism and the Radical 1960s*

Shirley Jennifer Lim, *Anna May Wong: Performing the Modern*

Edward Tang, *From Confinement to Containment: Japanese/American Arts during the Early Cold War*

Patricia P. Chu, *Where I Have Never Been: Migration, Melancholia, and Memory in Asian American Narratives of Return*

Cynthia Wu, *Sticky Rice: A Politics of Intraracial Desire*

Marguerite Nguyen, *America's Vietnam: The Longue Durée of U.S. Literature and Empire*

Vanita Reddy, *Fashioning Diaspora: Beauty, Femininity, and South Asian American Culture*

A list of additional titles in this series appears at the back of this book.

Prisoner of Wars

*A Hmong Fighter Pilot's
Story of Escaping Death
and Confronting Life*

CHIA YOUYEE VANG

with PAO YANG, *Retired Captain,
U.S. Secret War in Laos*

TEMPLE UNIVERSITY PRESS
Philadelphia • Rome • Tokyo

TEMPLE UNIVERSITY PRESS
Philadelphia, Pennsylvania 19122
tupress.temple.edu

Copyright © 2021 by Temple University—Of The Commonwealth System
  of Higher Education
All rights reserved
Published 2021

Note: Photos are from Pao and Ena's personal collection except where noted.
All photos from Laos and Thailand were given to them by family and friends
after they arrived in the United States.

Library of Congress Cataloging-in-Publication Data

Names: Vang, Chia Youyee, 1971– author. | Yang, Pao, approximately 1948–
Title: Prisoner of wars : a Hmong fighter pilot's story of escaping death
  and confronting life / Chia Youyee Vang, with Pao Yang, Retired Captain,
  U.S. Secret War in Laos.
Other titles: Asian American history and culture.
Description: Philadelphia : Temple University Press, 2021. | Series: Asian
  American history and culture | Includes bibliographical references and
  index. | Summary: "An oral history biography of Pao Yang, one of several
  dozen Hmong fighter pilots secretly trained by the United States Air Force
  during the Vietnam War. Recounts his capture, escape, and migration to the
  United States and challenges dominant paradigms of Asian American
  history and Southeast Asian refugees"—Provided by publisher.
Identifiers: LCCN 2020013138 (print) | LCCN 2020013139 (ebook) |
  ISBN 9781439919385 (cloth) | ISBN 9781439919392 (paperback) |
  ISBN 9781439919408 (pdf)
Subjects: LCSH: Yang, Pao, approximately 1948– | Air pilots, Military—
  Laos—Biography. | Vietnam War, 1961–1975—Participation, Hmong
  (Asian people) | Prisoners of war—Laos. | Hmong American families. |
  Hmong (Asian people)—United States. | LCGFT: Oral histories.
Classification: LCC UG626.2.Y365 V36 2021 (print) | LCC UG626.2.Y365
  (ebook) | DDC 959.704/37 [B]—dc23
LC record available at https://lccn.loc.gov/2020013138
LC ebook record available at https://lccn.loc.gov/2020013139

♾ The paper used in this publication meets the requirements of the
American National Standard for Information Sciences—Permanence of
Paper for Printed Library Materials, ANSI Z39.48-1992

Printed in the United States of America

9 8 7 6 5 4 3 2 1

To all prisoners of war who did not return to tell their stories.

Contents

Acknowledgments		*ix*
Introduction		*1*
1	"No One Returned for Me"	*15*
2	Early Life and the Quest for Knowledge	*27*
3	To Fly the Iron Eagle	*39*
4	Love and War	*49*
5	No Room for Mistakes	*59*
6	Prisoner of War	*65*
7	Precarious Freedom	*75*
8	Return from the Dead	*97*
9	A Second Chance	*109*
10	"I Lived to Tell My Story"	*133*
Notes		*139*
Bibliography		*143*
Index		*145*

Acknowledgments

Chia Youyee Vang

After our initial meeting in Winder, Georgia, during the summer of 2013, I returned to interview Pao Yang again in August 2015. The purpose was to gain a more complete understanding of his prison camp experiences and how that had a lasting impact on his life. I stayed with his family. In addition to Pao, I interviewed his current wife, Ena Yang (formerly known as Sinxai Moua), and I had the opportunity to meet two of his children, Vaug and Ta.

I am grateful that Pao has entrusted me to write this book. I appreciate his willingness to talk about dark moments in his life. I also thank Pao's current wife, Ena, and his first wife, Ong Moua, for allowing me to listen to their stories. Patriarchal social practices compounded by the unruly circumstances of war affected their young lives in extraordinary ways. Since I began the Hmong pilot oral history project in 2013, I have encountered many community members who expressed much curiosity about Pao's prisoner of war (POW) experiences and his relationship with Ong after he returned. Much had changed

ACKNOWLEDGMENTS

by the time Pao reached the refugee camps. Believing that Pao had died since he did not return after the 1973 cease-fire agreement, Ong remarried and immigrated to the United States. Prior to escaping from Laos, Pao married Ena. The complicated situation did not allow for Pao and Ong to go back to their original marriage after he arrived in the United States in 1979. Over the years, they have seen each other at extended family and community events, but the encounters were typically uncomfortable and at times tense. It is not my place to either pass judgment or offer any observations about their fractured lives, but as I listened to their reflections, I came away with a heavy burden compelling me to conclude that they have never had closure. The state of their family relationships reveal that decades of trauma have gone untreated, and it is not likely that any durable resolution will be achieved in the foreseeable future. My brief conversations with their adult children during my visits to interview the parents further suggests that it will take a miracle to bring peace to their parents' problematic disposition.

In spite of the challenges, I would like to note that this book would not have been possible without Ena's intense desire to see it written. I believe that she has her own reasons. She was a teenager when Pao and her parents arranged for her to marry him. She knew little of his background until the two of them had escaped to Thailand. The more she discovered about her husband's past, the more she desired for people to know what had happened to him during and after the war.

According to Pao and Ena, other people have been interested in writing Pao's biography, but none followed through. Ena could not have predicted the content of this book when she sat down with me to share her own story in 2015. Following my interview with her, I pointed out to Ena and Pao that it would be impossible for me to write this book without incorporating Ong's perspectives. They agreed and gave me Ong's number. A few weeks later, I made a separate trip to Georgia to interview her. At the time, Ong lived with her eldest son, Pheng, and his wife. They generously allowed me to stay at their home, where I conducted Ong's interview.

This book includes specific, compelling aspects of Pao Yang's life and by no means represents a thorough, chronological listing of everything he did. The story is narrated primarily by Pao, with brief recollections from others in his life. My role was to document their lived experiences and then intersperse the narrative with important historical events to provide context. I have chosen to primarily focus on Pao's journey as a POW while omitting certain intimate and dramatic episodes that remain highly emotional for members of his family, who are, after all, still living the legacy of Pao's wartime experiences. I do not believe the omitted details are necessary to this already complex narrative. Consequently, this book overwhelmingly reflects the interpretations of Pao and his generation regarding their lives. Pao's voice is conveyed by way of direct quotations, as—to a lesser extent—are the voices of Ena and Ong. While I also had brief conversations with Pao's older children (Pheng Yang, Ta Xiong, and Vaug Yang), as mentioned previously, family dynamics influenced my decision to limit inclusion of their perspectives for this biography. I conducted telephone interviews with Pao's relative Chee Yang in August 2015 to learn his perspective regarding what happened at Long Cheng following Pao's capture and with Pao's fellow prisoner Nhia Yee Thao (Nyaj Yig Thoj) about his recollection of Pao at the prison camp. Upon completion of the draft manuscript, I returned to Pao's home in Georgia on March 29, 2018. I read the entire manuscript to him and Ena. I also met with Ong and read to her the parts of this book that mentioned her. To honor Pao for allowing me to document and share his life story, I decided to list him as my coauthor.

I am grateful to several individuals at Temple University Press. Former editor Sara Cohen had reached out to me regarding another project. When I shared with her my draft of Pao's

ACKNOWLEDGMENTS

biography, she believed that it was a compelling story and forwarded it to series editor Shelley Lee. The thoughtful feedback that both provided was instrumental in shaping the manuscript. I thank the anonymous reviewers who expressed enthusiasm for the project's potential contribution to the literature and offered detailed guidance to strengthen it. My gratitude extends to Sarah Munroe, who assumed charge of the project following Sara Cohen's departure, and Shaun Vigil, who became editor after Sarah Monroe left the press.

I continue to feel extremely blessed to be a part of an institution that supports my research. The many trips to conduct interviews for the larger oral history project benefited from resources that the University of Wisconsin–Milwaukee provides to the Hmong Diaspora Studies Program that I founded in 2009. Since 2013, the funding has enabled me to involve six students. In addition to serving as my program assistant, Rebekah Bain prepared the index. Finally, I appreciate that my husband, Tong Mabyias Yang, and my children, Simone, Tujntsuj, and Flasche, were willing to come along on research trips. Thank you, Tong, for reading the numerous versions and engaging in many conversations about the content. All contributions aside, I alone accept responsibility for any shortcomings in this work.

Pao (Tswv Cheem) Yang

Ua ntej no kuv thov ua tsaug rau ib tsoom phooj ywg nrog rau ib tsoom tub ntxhais hluas uas nej xav nyeem thiab xav paub txog kuv lub neej. Nej txhua leej txhua tus yuav tau nyeem txog kuv lub neej uas yog qhov tseeb tiag tsis yog cuav tsis yog txua (I am grateful to friends and the younger generation for your interest in my life. What you will read is based on my experiences and how I remember them. It is not merely a story. They are my truths).

xii

Prisoner of Wars

Introduction

This book is the product of encounters that people have with others as they try to make sense of life's twists and turns. It is a story about human beings' will to survive at all costs. More specifically, it reveals the trials and tribulations that people across the globe have endured as part of twentieth-century global political and military struggles generally, and U.S.-Asia relations specifically. Exploring how a young Hmong man navigated through wartime Laos to become a fighter pilot who subsequently served as a prisoner of war (POW) before seeking refuge in the United States makes visible an aspect of the collateral damage that has been left out of dominant Vietnam War narratives.

I first met Pao Yang in July 2013 while conducting oral history interviews with Hmong veterans regarding their experiences relating to the U.S. Secret War in Laos. Several months earlier, I had been asked by a group of Hmong pilot veterans to assist them in documenting their involvement in a secret aviation training program, codenamed Water Pump, that the U.S. Air Force (USAF) and the Central Intelligence Agency

(CIA) established during the war. During the summer of 2013, I traveled throughout the United States to interview former Hmong pilots, U.S. intelligence personnel, USAF instructors who taught them how to fly, American pilots who flew with them, and family members of pilots killed in action.[1] As part of this project, I met with Pao at his home in Winder, Georgia. Unlike most of his fellow surviving pilots, Pao was unable to leave Laos in 1975. His T-28D aircraft was shot down during a bombing mission in June 1972. He survived but was captured by enemy forces and sent to a jungle POW camp in northeastern Laos. Unlike American POWs, Pao was not released in 1973 following the cease-fire agreements. The high crime that he committed was having fought on the American side. He remained imprisoned for three years after the United States withdrew from Vietnam. The story of thousands like Pao who contributed to U.S. military efforts during the Vietnam War would have been completely erased if nearly 150,000 of their ethnic group had not fled Laos and resettled as political refugees in the United States.

Who are the Hmong, and how did they become entangled in the Vietnam War? The Hmong are an ethnic group with origins in southern China, where today an estimated five million reside. They are one of several groups that make up the Miao nationality. Scholars agree that their migration to the Indochinese Peninsula occurred in significant numbers beginning in the mid- to late 1800s.[2] Their migration took place during a turbulent time for the Chinese Empire, when large numbers of Chinese emigrated abroad.[3] Political and economic factors motivated the exodus of those who called themselves Hmong.[4] The migrants set down roots in the northern mountainous regions in what are the present-day countries of Vietnam, Laos, and Thailand, and they survived on subsistence farming far removed from ruling powers.[5] Isolation from the larger societies in which they lived, however, failed to prevent them from being enmeshed in nineteenth- and twentieth-century political and military confrontations. Rather, European colonialism and U.S. imperial projects forced them to become involved.

French colonial administrators introduced Hmong in Laos to their first experience of the benefits of aligning with an imperial power. The French carried out the practice of divide and conquer so that division occurred between the Hmong as clans competed to represent Hmong interests to the colonial regime.[6] Hmong often found themselves on opposite sides during anticolonial struggles. This contentious situation further expanded as French colonial rule in Indochina ended in 1954 and U.S. interests in the region increased due to the growing Cold War.[7]

Laos was pulled into the war within this context of greater American military buildup in Vietnam largely because President Dwight Eisenhower believed that Laos was key to the entire Southeast Asia region.[8] Laos shares its eastern border with Vietnam. Thus, both U.S. and Vietnamese communist forces used Lao territory to enhance their war efforts in Vietnam. A concurrent civil war between Lao neutralists and communists, the Pathet Lao, divided this newly independent nation and propelled the warring factions to accept outside military aid. What eventually came to be known as the U.S. Secret War in Laos was directly influenced by political and military decisions regarding Vietnam. U.S. bases sprang up in Thailand between 1950 and 1975 to serve as staging grounds against communist forces in the region.

In an effort to ensure Laos would be a noncommunist country, the U.S. Operations Mission launched numerous Lao nation-building efforts in the mid- to late 1950s. The Royal Lao Government under Prince Souvanna Phouma became the recipient of significant American aid. A Military Assistance and Advisory Group (MAAG) was established for Laos in 1955. In the process of strengthening the Royal Lao Army (RLA), the country was divided into five military regions. In 1959, North Vietnamese leaders decided to support southern revolutionaries' armed resistance against the U.S.-sponsored regime. MAAG advisors determined that ground forces were needed, resulting in the increase of Lao men to serve in the U.S.-financed RLA and recruitment of Hmong and other ethnic minority groups who lived near the Laos-Vietnam border. In January 1961, then-colonel Harry Aderholt and CIA officer Colonel James William "Bill" Lair met with Major Vang Pao, who was the only ethnic minority military officer of Hmong descent. Many Hmong fought on the side of the French during the First Indochina War and were regarded as good fighters in the mountainous terrain. The two Americans had heard of Vang Pao's reputation of successfully leading troops against the Vietminh forces. At the time, he was in charge of Laos's Military Region II, located in the northeastern part of the country bordering northern Vietnam. The meeting was to try to lure the Hmong to the noncommunist side.[9] Following this encounter, the CIA proceeded to establish Operation Momentum to secretly arm and train Hmong under Vang Pao. Bill Lair planned the operation, in which training would be carried out by a small number of CIA and U.S. Army Special Forces Mobile Training Teams (MTTs) alongside members of the Thai Police Aerial Reinforcement Unit, which he founded. Enlistment of Hmong men began after the meeting and weapons and supplies soon arrived.

By the mid-1960s, the United States was fully financing all pro-American factions within Laos via Thailand. Unlike in Vietnam, where nearly three million American soldiers served, in Laos the country's neutrality meant that no American combat troops were sent there. Indigenous forces became America's foot soldiers. Ground troops were instrumental in engaging with Lao and Vietnamese communist forces, but air support provided by American and Thai pilots was risky. Thus, the strengthening of Royal Lao Army air capacity was also necessary.

Before France departed in 1955, it had established a small aerial and support arm for the army referred to as Aviation Laotiènne (Lao Aviation). The United States transformed it into the Royal Lao Air Force in 1960, but air capability was absent.

With U.S. support, twenty pilot trainees graduated from an eleven-month program in 1962; however, they were only able to fly observation aircraft.[10] American and some Thai pilots flew missions in Laos, but since this was in violation of Lao neutrality, Lao leaders advocated for training Lao men to become fighter pilots. Thus, the Water Pump Program was created in 1964.[11]

Water Pump consisted of a T-28 maintenance and training facility at Udorn Royal Thai Air Force Base using equipment from the CIA's airline, Air America. Initially, only Lao students were allowed to join American and Thai pilots who were also learning to become T-28 qualified. Americans were the primary instructors, but in 1969, two Lao individuals were upgraded to instructor pilots (IPs).

While Military Region II saw some of the most intense fighting, Hmong men were initially not allowed to train as fighter pilots. Most American and Lao leaders did not support their participation due to prevalent stereotypes about Hmong as "illiterate hill tribesmen" and "savages." Because of the dominant role that the CIA played in Laotian affairs, however, the first two Hmong students were admitted to Water Pump in 1966. Despite the stereotypes that American IPs were told upon coming to the program, some changed their views about their students after they began working with them.

From 1966 to 1974, nearly fifty Hmong men learned how to fly aircraft, of which thirty-eight graduated. Thirty-two graduated from T-28 training and joined other Lao pilots working under the call sign for the T-28 pilots, Chao Pha Khao. Of the thirty-eight pilots, seventeen were killed in action. Over the course of the war, the Hmong clandestine army consisted of about forty thousand troops and estimates of combatant casualties range from seventeen thousand to thirty-five thousand. The pilots who survived were among the thousands who resettled as political refugees in the Western Hemisphere. Twenty pilots sought refuge in the United States and one in France.

INTRODUCTION

Because of the secretive nature of the Water Pump Program, few people were aware of its details at the time—or even today. As a CIA covert operation, the program was hidden from historical accounts. Most of the surviving pilots settled quietly in the United States and did their best to move on with their new lives. It was not until 2010 that the U.S. Air Force officially recognized one of the pilots at the Pentagon Airmen Hall. Two years later, the former pilots held a reunion in Minnesota. Most saw each other at this reunion for the first time since they left the Thai refugee camps in the mid-1970s. After the 2012 reunion, the reunion organizing committee decided to find a way to document the pilots' wartime sacrifices, and a year later, I was asked to assist them with an oral history study due to my prior work on the Hmong diaspora. When I began this project, oral history was the necessary methodology since the voices and experiences of the people I was studying were not available in the archives. From such locations as Worcester, Massachusetts; Denver, Pennsylvania; Chesnee, South Carolina; Winder, Georgia; Plainfield, Illinois; Santa Rosa Beach, Florida; Meridian, Texas; and Fresno and Santa Ana, California, I asked interviewees to reflect on their wartime and postwar experiences.

Although the experiences of all interviewees in the larger study are worthy of greater attention, none compares to that of Pao Yang. His whirlwind life is an impactful illustration of the possibilities that existed at the time for a humble Hmong of rural background to gain access to the U.S.-sponsored military bureaucracy. His life provides a unique lens through which to better understand the lasting impact of the wars in Southeast Asia and to make visible the diverse journeys that migrants from Asia made over the last two centuries. As people of Asian descent who arrived after the social movements of the 1960s, Hmong benefited from the more positive perspectives on Asian Americans, but their primarily agrarian background with limited formal education contributed to a difficult start in the United States. More specifically, their inability to fit into the

6

INTRODUCTION

Asian American model minority category placed them in a precarious position. In other words, Asian American success had transformed their group from the unassimilable "yellow peril" to the model minority against which other minority groups are measured.[12] Hmong refugees frequently became study subjects largely due to their struggles with adjusting to life in an advanced society. Interestingly, however, many Americans know little about what set in motion Hmong forced migration to the United States in the mid-1970s.

Centuries of displacement in search of a permanent place to settle thrusted them into the fold of global political and military confrontations. Once entangled, they could no longer choose to be uninvolved. Like a fish who took the bait, the Hmong in Laos who sided with pro-American forces during the Vietnam War could not break free. They risked their lives because they believed then that they were on the right side of history under the wings of the great U.S. nation. Defeat was unimaginable, so they allowed their men and boys to transform from hill farmers to America's foot soldiers in a war that was decided by the political calculations of politicians on the other side of the globe. In the immediate postwar moment, they hoped to wake up from this nightmare, but they soon realized that this was not an option. It was, in fact, a tragic reality.

Through Pao's life story, this book weaves together important historical events that engulfed Hmong in Southeast Asia and their subsequent displacement to the Western Hemisphere. The deeply personal struggles that his family experienced in the United States opened up opportunities for them to reevaluate the "gift of freedom," as Mimi Thi Nguyen eloquently articulated, that had been forced upon them, as with other refugees.[13] Although the majority of the book takes place before Pao's arrival in the United States, it contributes to the literature on Asian American history in that it illustrates how Asian migration to this country has historically been intimately tied to U.S. imperial interests in Asia. Pao's life story enriches what

7

INTRODUCTION

we know about these processes throughout the twentieth century. Despite the vast literature on the Vietnam War, no other similar work exists that critically explores in-depth a Hmong veteran's experiences before, during, and after the war. The existing literature tends to focus on the perspectives of high-ranking officers, and they are generally celebratory. Pao's life story and critical reflections broaden our understanding of the impact that the war had on combatants and their families. Furthermore, his involvement with processing refugee resettlement cases provides insights into the international humanitarian bureaucracy, and thus, this book contributes to refugee and immigration studies. Moreover, it demonstrates the important role that oral history plays in broadening our understanding of historical events.

Pao Yang's memories as recorded in *Prisoner of Wars* underline the value of oral histories and personal experiences woven within the fabric of a larger and often complex historical narrative. As such, oral history contributes to the historical process by allowing historians to fill in gaps in the historical narrative that is by no means clear or complete, as limited records survive while others have disappeared from memory as completely as events that had never been recorded. Katherine Bowie likens oral histories to the art of pointillism, in which each dot contributes detail to an overall complex image.[14] Each oral history, or dot, contains merit and significance alone as unique, but when viewed within the context of other pieces of historical memory, an overall pattern emerges from which the learner can make meaning. But as with pointillism, the spaces between are blank, not filled in; so, too, is the twenty-first century's picture of the past. The historian can rely on the primary sources left behind in archives and on the scholarship of others, but a composite and ultimate history is impossible to reconstruct. Pao's story contributes to a more complete historical narrative of the Vietnam War. It is through oral histories that understudied and forgotten experiences previously regarded as immaterial in the past can come to the forefront.

The use of oral histories saw a significant rise in the 1960s and afterward, as historians turned their attention toward understanding the pasts of those previously believed to be insignificant.[15] Archives reflect these biases, revealed by what has been preserved within the repositories. A new emphasis on oral history allows history to become more democratic, recording and preserving the experiences of the community as well as society's influential.[16] The usage of a wide spectrum of personal experiences and memories "challenge historiographical paradigms," opening the door to new historical interpretations provided through a unique form of evidence.[17] This book demonstrates how Pao's story works to balance the existing literature that focuses on high-ranking officers that are of a generally celebratory nature. Oral histories provide a new form of documentary evidence that opens "new areas of inquiry" because of a lack of sources.[18] Pao's memories are particularly useful, as memories of the U.S. Secret War in Laos are limited, due to its covert nature. These "qualitative sources" provide access to materials for historians to investigate new social phenomena from differing viewpoints.[19] These newer areas of exploration include the intricate aspects of life that are easy to ignore, "such as personal relationships, domestic life, and the nature of clandestine organizations."[20] The reader can see these human traits within Pao's memories of his subsequent "wars" even after the official Vietnam War had ended. In addition, the inclusion of Pao's family members' voices within *Prisoner of Wars* reveals the thoughts and experiences of Hmong noncombatants whose lives were also affected greatly by these conflicts.

The element of relationship within any oral history is vital to consider, as it involves layers of context and complexity to the narrative. William Schneider shows that these stories were told to a specific person during a unique and particular time

INTRODUCTION

and place, all of which influenced the interviewee. He writes that the interviewer's "background, experiences, interests, and relationships with other community members are critical to motivating narrators to share their knowledge."[21] The relationship between the speaker and the interviewer is a matter of "intersubjectivity," through which the recollections are mediated and influenced by the perspectives of both parties.[22] My position as a coethnic with similar migration experiences, in addition to my role as a scholar with the ability to not only learn from but also capture and share their experiences with others, persuaded Pao, Ena, and Ong to answer my questions. Also shaping the discourse is the relationship between the narrator and the wider community, whether present or past; the lens through which the speaker views past experiences involves the individual's relationship with wider society. Furthermore, while listening to an oral history or reading its transcript, a relationship is built between the subject and the learner in a way no other historical source can provide. The reader experiences the past in the voice of one who experienced it firsthand as a witness to history itself, which allows the reader a personal connection to the past, "break[ing] down barriers" of mediation through layers of third-person historians and editors.[23] By opening up about the sadness that had plagued their lives for decades, Pao, Ena, and Ong—the three main narrators of this oral history—are given some agency in influencing how society should understand their predicament.

Due to the nature of oral history as a direct voice of a witness of the past to the reader, oral histories have a unique emotional ingredient to them that is missing in other forms of historical sources. Mark Cave outlines the use of oral history as a "blueprint for further historical inquiry as well as a baseline of emotional perspective."[24] Other forms of primary sources lack this emotional perspective of someone experiencing an event firsthand. Emotion plays a complicated role within history, as it influences events, relationships, and viewpoints, yet is often

10

INTRODUCTION

overlooked because of the difficulty measuring and gauging an accurate and concrete picture of individual and collective feelings. Yet "emotion is a big part of truth, particularly in times of crisis."[25] Cave describes the role of emotion as the "complexities of the human heart and mind," which is indeed a piece of history itself.[26] Already a complex element of human history, emotion is further convoluted in times of tragedy and hardship. A community traumatized by war has its experiences and past so intertwined with the volatile emotions accompanying the era that history and human feeling are impossible to detach from one another. Even so, the latter is often overlooked by historians in favor of hard facts and statistics, which creates an imbalanced picture of a situation. Elena Poniatowska articulates that oral history mitigates this discrepancy by allowing the living witnesses' voices to be "intertwined to make up the unique and plural voice of the anonymous suffering mass, the voice of those who have no voice."[27]

Criticism of the format of oral histories and their use within the arc of history usually revolves around their subjective and personal nature. After all, emotion is not widespread and equal across an entire society but is unique to the individual. Likewise, each individual has an interpretation of events and a worldview lens through which to analyze the past, and these biases are inherent within oral histories. Other critics worry about how memories warp and change over time, possibly producing an inaccurate representation of history. William Schneider writes that interviewees create a story narrative format out of their memories by "choosing out of the myriad of possibilities which things to share in story and how to say it."[28] *Prisoner of Wars* acknowledges this difficulty in creating a coherent narrative over the course of the conflict in Southeast Asia. However, Alistair Thomson views the unreliability of memory as "a resource, rather than a problem, for historical interpretation and reconstruction."[29] Oral history pioneer Paul Thompson concurs, writing that these "life experience[s] . . . can be used as its

INTRODUCTION

raw material," providing a "new dimension . . . to history." After all, "reality is complex and many-sided," and these personal sides within the oral histories contribute to understanding how those who experienced events firsthand understood them, felt about them, and produced meaning for an event.[30]

This process of creating meaning out of historical events is done consciously or subconsciously by everyone, including historians. The ways the interviewee processes life experiences into meaningful events is an important tool for researchers to explore the complex layers of past interpretations and viewpoints on contemporary events. Lynn Abrams reveals the twofold nature of memory in oral histories, both of individual and collective memories formed by a single person and the wider community.[31] The former seeks to produce a "sense of self" within the context of past occurrences.[32] The latter fits within Cave's assertion that the "process of meaningful remembrance is a social process" that is built on their cultural environments.[33] The oral histories themselves are then meant to "convey meaning to others" in wider society.[34] Abrams sees these processes of remembrance and meaning as a way for individuals and collective communities to create order out of disorder, as historical events are often messy and filled with confusion.[35]

The record of Pao Yang's experiences as a Hmong fighter pilot as illustrated in *Prisoner of Wars* illustrates the need for further work in the field of oral history. The loss of Pao's memories would have resulted in a continued historical silence on Hmong prisoners of war, but through his own words, the reader has a new understanding of the experiences of both an individual fighter pilot and the larger Hmong community. Oral histories bring new perspectives and understandings to light that were not given prominent attention in past historiography. Pao describes his gracious contribution to historical scholarship as "not merely a story. These are my truths."

I chose the title because it fully captures how Pao describes the many struggles he confronted before and after he physically

12

served time as a POW. Although the book relies on Pao's recollections, it is neither a traditional biography nor an autobiography. A biography is an account of a person's life that is written by another person, whereas an autobiography is an account of a person's life written by that person. *Prisoner of Wars* is a blending of the two approaches. It relies on Pao's recollections, but as the main author, I provide the historical context that is necessary to understand Pao's experiences before and after he arrived in the United States. The narrative is not chronological. Instead, it traverses between different parts of his past. Chapter 1 opens with events that unfolded the day Pao's aircraft was shot down and the factors that contributed to why he was not rescued. Due to the financial benefits and prestige of being a pilot, landing a spot on the roster of pilot trainees required a certain level of formal education and political maneuvering. Pao's early life experiences and the paths that he followed to obtain formal education are discussed in Chapter 2, followed by his aviation training in Chapter 3, which also gives us a glimpse into the treatment of Hmong pilot trainees by Lao, Thai, and American officers and instructors.

The existing scholarship on Hmong involvement in the war in Laos has focused predominantly on men's military contributions. Chapter 4 details the complex love story between Pao and his first wife and sheds light on the war's enormous impact on women, who often could not focus on daily activities while their spouses went on bombing missions. The dangerous topography in addition to the low-quality aircraft provided to Laos often left no room for mistakes, as illustrated in Chapter 5. Chapter 6 exposes us to Pao's gruesome experience in POW camp, and Chapter 7 explores his precarious freedom following his release and the conditions that facilitated his escape. Believed to have been killed, Pao's escape across the Lao/Thai border was described as him having returned from the dead. Chapter 8 recounts the emotional reunion with family and fellow community members in the refugee camp. It also divulges the difficult

INTRODUCTION

decisions that displaced people had to make. Chapter 9 traces key moments in Pao's efforts to rebuild his life in the United States. Although he found freedom, trauma became an integral part of his life. The deeply personal account allows readers to follow the journey of a man who had escaped death only to find himself unable to return to the life that he had left behind. In Chapter 10, Pao reflects on the process of remembering old wounds and accepting the things that he could not control during the course of living.

14

1

"No One Returned for Me"

Having provided close air support to ground troops for about six months, Pao Yang's aircraft had been hit many times. He had grown accustomed to seeing holes all over the aircraft after he landed. Each time he was relieved to have escaped death. The bomber T-28D model Chao Pha Khao pilots flew was a modified T-28A training aircraft. It enabled Hmong and Lao pilots to fly near treetops, which increased bombing accuracy. The close air support capability of Chao Pha Khao pilots overwhelmed enemy forces at the same time that it put the pilots in great danger.

The enemy usually reserved the Soviet 37 mm antiaircraft artillery guns for American jets flying high. Its length and weight made it difficult to quickly move the gun and point it at the target. Since the T-28D pilots flew very low, the enemy used the 12.8 mm and 12.7 mm instead. "When I was hit," Pao recounted, "it was from a 12.8 mm. It was because I was not lucky that day. Something was said to be wrong with my plane and the mechanics couldn't figure it out. Just as I was about to go home, they said they had fixed it." He climbed into the air-

CHAPTER 1

craft to join his fellow pilots, Koua Xiong and John Bounchanh Sayavong, on an urgent mission.[1] The three would be led by an ethnic Lao pilot named Kongthong, whose last name Pao does not remember. After the four 250-pound bombs were securely loaded, he followed the other pilots in hot pursuit of the enemy as he had done in nearly one thousand other missions. He dropped the first, second, and third bombs and told himself, "One more, then I would be on my way home!"[2]

That would not be the case. "But just at that last moment before dropping the bomb, my plane was hit. I heard a huge noise under my feet. [The plane] quickly caught on fire and dropped headfirst. My hair curled up, and I could feel fire surrounding my face. I couldn't open my eyes." If the fire had started on the wings or another part of the plane, he believes he would have been able to guide it to friendly territory.

Because the plane was on fire, his immediate response was to press the parachute button. "At that moment, it was horrible! I was in a daze because of the fire, plus, when the parachute ejected, it jerked me. Since I had just been hovering over enemy troops, it took a very short time for me to reach the ground." Pao's aircraft fell right next to the enemy's camp in an area known to the Hmong as Thai Dia Choua (Thaib Dhia Tsua). In northeastern Laos, where the mountains are grandiose, he considered himself fortunate to have not smashed onto the mountainside. A number of pilots were killed when thick fog blocked their view of mountains that seemed to have emerged from nowhere. The problems were not only due to the mountainous terrain. The T-28D were poor-quality aircraft that were no longer used in Vietnam. Instead of discontinuing them, U.S. civilian and military officials decided to transfer them to be used in Laos without regard for the safety of local pilots and the American volunteers who flew with them.

Pao explained with much frustration, "This is on the side called Na Mai (Naj Maib). There were communist Vietnamese only. No communist Lao. Vietnamese only. They brought their

16

large guns to that mountain range to shoot at our soldiers, very heavy artillery. We had some soldiers at Phou Long Math (Phu Loos Maj) and some at Phou Pha Xai (Phuj Phaj Xai). The leaders told the pilots that we had to go bomb those guns. We had enough communist forces to deal with around Long Cheng, and we couldn't even get to them all! But still, they told us to go bomb this heavily armed area. That's how I was shot down!"

Long Cheng was the location where the CIA established its operation with General Vang Pao. From the early 1960s to the mid-1970s, the CIA worked with Hmong to transform the densely forested valley to a lively town of nearly forty thousand inhabitants. Its population grew dramatically due to the relocation of people who could not remain in their villages. Long Cheng was not like Saigon or other cities and towns with U.S. troop presence. At any point, there would be only a few CIA operatives and other American intelligence officers orchestrating military and humanitarian activities. With readily available aircraft to fly them back to the capital city, Vientiane, Americans who served in Laos typically did not stay overnight. As the CIA's headquarters, it was the frequent target of enemy fire and communist troops had attempted to overrun it many times.

Pao remembers that fateful moment when he hit the ground. "I could hear them screaming and surrounding me, but because my pilot friends flew very low overhead to give me cover, they did not approach me right away." Years later, when he saw Koua Xiong and John Bounchanh Sayavong in the United States, Pao learned from his fellow pilots that he was almost rescued. In their T-28D aircraft, they provided cover as a helicopter, which had just dropped off water at Padong, a nearby town, attempted the rescue. Koua and Bounchanh were soon forced to leave the scene because they were running out of fuel. Said Pao, "A rope was dropped, and it almost reached me. However, because of heavy fire, the helicopter was hit many times, [and] the pilot [also] left. They said that the helicopter was almost shot down near me. So, with that there was no more time to rescue

CHAPTER 1

me, and the enemy surrounded me." The soldiers pulled him and the parachute into the cave in which they had been hiding. Shooting down a T-28D aircraft was considered a success for the communist troops since the pilots often inflicted great damage on them. Those whose aircraft were shot down during bombing missions typically died. Pao was one of only two from Military Region II who managed to survive. Bounchanh continued to fly following Pao's capture. During one mission, enemy antiartillery guns shot down Bounchanh's T-28D. He was able to turn his aircraft away from the enemy camp and parachuted to safety. Although he was severely injured, the rescue attempt to retrieve him succeeded.

For years, Pao had mulled over the issue of why he was not rescued. He told himself that it was a dangerous situation because the enemy had captured him shortly after he hit the ground. When he mentioned the enemy in our conversations, he was referring to both the Pathet Lao and their Vietnamese communist supporters. He often emphasized the enemy as *nyab laj* (Vietnamese). In his mind, the fact that it was Vietnamese soldiers who captured him further magnified the dominant role that they played in Pathet Lao affairs. Regarding why he was not rescued, Pao further justified that General Vang Pao and his CIA advisors likely calculated the risks and decided not to attempt further rescue missions. But deep down inside, the pain of being forgotten persists, primarily because he had been around long enough to see how those in power valued lives differently. "I was left in enemy hands because the leaders did not send rescue airplanes for me. What they did send was not even a pilot rescue helicopter! It was a very slow helicopter with no gunship. We've seen rescue efforts for American pilots. There were fighter jets and helicopters with gunship[s] to rescue downed American pilots. My rescue did not include any of that!" Why did General Vang Pao and his officers not treat Pao the same as American pilots? Why did they not utilize the same resources to rescue him? He had legitimate reasons to question the differences.

18

"NO ONE RETURNED FOR ME"

Pao described the situation with a Hmong saying that he felt better explained Vang Pao's actions: "'Pulling one hair is not going to make you bald.' So, even if I died, it wouldn't matter to them. It doesn't hurt them. Our Hmong way of war was based on factionalism. If you did not have a close relative in a powerful position who could forcefully say that you had to be rescued at all costs, then it would not happen. I didn't have a powerful brother or uncle, and that was why there weren't those rescue planes for me. No fighter jets and helicopters to rescue me. My friends covered me for as long as they could before they retreated. That was it. No one returned for me!" Nepotism among Hmong leaders helps to explain how different members of the clandestine army were treated, but from a broader point of view, when a Hmong pilot was shot down, Hmong leaders did not have the power to expend the resources used when an American pilot was. Since the United States was operating under the pretense that it was not officially in Laos, U.S. military leaders were motivated to rescue downed American pilots at all costs to avoid enemy forces capturing them, which would provide evidence of American presence there. Local pilots, on the other hand, were likely regarded as dispensable.

By 1972, communist forces had moved so close to the Long Cheng area that aircraft had to take off from the Laotian capital of Vientiane, eighty miles southwest of Long Cheng. Due to Pao's pilot salary, his family was able to rent a house there. His mother lived with Pao, Ong, and their son, Pheng, whereas Pao's father came and went between this home and his home with his other wife. Polygamy was an accepted practice, and it increased significantly during the war, when so many men were killed. The wealth that some Hmong men gained from the U.S.-sponsored military also contributed to many marrying multiple wives. Reflecting on that fateful day, June 10, 1972, Pao's first wife, Ong Moua, explained, "I had cried and begged him to go fly one day and then stay home for a day before going back to fly. He'd always say that work is work. On that day, it

19

CHAPTER 1

was his day to rest. I don't know if he told you everything. It was his day to rest and not work. But, that day, we had planned to go find a cow to have a soul calling (hu plig) ceremony for our son, Pheng. Since it was his day to rest, I did ask him not to go to the office. He replied, '*Me pli* [my spirit], you worry too much. OK, today I will stay with you. After breakfast, we will go have some fun at Thadeua [Road] and then go look for a cow so that tomorrow we can have the soul calling ceremony for our child.' When I got out of bed, he followed and began to get dressed. I asked him why he was getting dressed [in his work clothes] when it was his day off. He was afraid of me asking him, but he responded that even though it was his day off, he had not talked to his superiors. He told me to get dressed and he would drop me off at the market to get something to eat while he quickly went to check in with them. He'd then come right back to pick me up, and after breakfast we would go have fun all day at Thadeua. We'd go find a cow before nightfall."[3] Hmong believe that a soul calling ceremony is important to ensure the child's good health physically and spiritually. Ong had wanted to have the ceremony for weeks, but Pao's schedule would not allow it. Thus, his suggestion pleased her greatly.

Pilots on duty between 1968 and 1970 were very busy. This was the case because of heightened activities in the larger Vietnam War. The year 1968 saw the highest number of U.S. troops in Vietnam (more than 530,000). It was also when the infamous Tet Offense and My Lai massacre took place. In the former, North Vietnamese and their allies in the south carried out surprise attacks throughout South Vietnam that changed Americans' views of how the war was going. Although the nature of the latter would not be exposed until 1969, it also had a dramatic impact on support for the war at home and abroad. These periods of heavy fighting in Vietnam affected the work of Hmong pilots. They would leave early in the morning and not return until evening. By early 1972, when Pao was on active duty, diplomacy was taking place publicly and privately between the United States and North Vietnam. On the Lao side, the different factions increased efforts to gain territorial dominance. Consequently, the Hmong pilots were extremely busy. Family members rarely spent quality time with them. That was why Ong had wanted to have the ceremony on that day. Thrilled with Pao's revised plan for their day together, she hopped on the back of his motorbike, and they cruised toward the Morning Market (Talat Sao). He dropped her off and then went straight to the airport office. Ong recalled, "I walked around the market and bought vegetables. When he dropped me off, it was only 7:30 A.M. I waited until 9:00 A.M. He didn't return. It was 9:15 A.M., and he still wasn't back. By then, I was frantically worried. My heart was beating so fast. I was crying inside. I couldn't wait any longer, so I decided to take a taxi home. I told myself that if he came to look for me and couldn't find me, I'd apologize later."

When she arrived at the house, the elders were waiting for her as they usually did. The rice was cooked, so she quickly prepared the vegetables. Ong continued, "I boiled some of the greens in one pot, and in another pot, I mixed some chicken with mustard green. When it was ready, I told my mother-in-law that they should go ahead and eat. As usual, she asked why I wasn't eating, and I responded that I was waiting for my husband to return to eat. So, I asked her to slowly eat and feed Pheng. It was now almost 10:00 A.M., so I went to take a shower because it was really hot. I took a quick shower, put on my panties, and wrapped a sarong around me. At that moment, I heard a motorbike approach the house. I was so happy! I thought to myself, 'My husband is back!' I exited the bathroom. I didn't understand why I had not yet heard him speak. Every day when he returned, he would immediately talk to the children outside. [He would usually ask] his younger sister, 'Where's your sister-in-law?' I was always the first person he looked for."

CHAPTER 1

Ong had expected to hear Pao's voice. When she did not hear him speak, she realized that the sound was not that of his motorbike. "My heart sank! [Pilot] Vang Seng was already parked outside of the house. I went outside with no shoes and shirt. Just my sarong. When he saw me, it seemed like he couldn't find any words to say. He didn't say anything. I asked him, 'Brother Seng, why are you here? What do you have to tell me?' Without realizing it, I was already hitting him with my fists. He was still sitting on the bike with his helmet on. He took off his helmet and said that whatever spirits we needed to call, we should because Coy—Pao was skinny so they called him Coy ["skinny" in Lao language]—was shot down about 8:20 or 8:30 A.M. He also said that they had not heard of any announcements, so we should call the spirits." For Hmong who practice ancestral worship, it is common to seek the help of their ancestors' spirits to guide whatever situation to a positive outcome. This often involves the promise to repay the spirits at a future date. Burning of incense and joss paper and sacrificing animals typically constitute the payments.

Vang Seng's message was not the news Ong had wanted to hear. She wanted him to tell her that everything would be all right and that Pao would be home soon. "At that moment, I didn't know what to do. I became numb. I couldn't cry. I couldn't scream. I couldn't say anything. After the message, Vang Seng got ready to leave while my father-in-law grabbed some incense to burn. Without realizing what I was doing, I climbed on the back of Vang Seng's motorbike. He turned around and asked what I thought I was doing. I was like a mute. I couldn't speak. All I heard was my mother-in-law saying that I should let go because the bike might fall. Vang Seng didn't know what to say, so he rode back to the airport with me." Normally the trip would be less than half an hour, but this time, it seemed like an eternity to Ong. Halfway there, she closed her eyes and held on to Vang Seng tightly, for she feared that she would pass out and fall off the motorbike. She thought

22

about Pao's promise to return for her at the market. For a brief moment, she was angry that he did not keep his promise. Why did he have to fly today? It was his day off, so why did another pilot not go on this mission instead? As these thoughts went through her mind over and over again, she felt the motorbike slow down and eventually come to a complete halt.

They had arrived at the Wattay airport. She quickly opened her eyes and slid off the motorbike. As she glanced around, she saw Pao's motorbike. She then quickly turned toward the aircraft parking lot and noticed that his T-28D was gone. It was at this moment that she cried loudly. Ong remembers the men trying to calm her down. When Vang Seng's superiors, a Lao commander and an American officer, were told that Pao Yang's wife had arrived, they came to talk to her. "The Lao commander who oversaw the operation held me and said that he was sorry that Pao was shot down but that Pao was able to radio to them so I shouldn't worry. He was still alive. He told me that they were in communication with him and that they already [had] two rescue helicopters searching for Pao. The American spoke Thai and asked me if I understood Thai. I said that I only knew very little so he would have to speak slowly. He said that I should not be afraid and for me to stay calm. They had already sent two helicopters to look for Pao."

In actuality, the officers were merely trying to ease her fears. Only one helicopter attempted to rescue Pao. Although he did try to use his radio after he had hit the ground, it did not work. As he explained, "I grabbed my radio and spoke into it, 'Chao Pha Khao, do you hear me?' Only complete silence!" No communication with Pao ever took place after he parachuted. Since Ong did not know about this at the time, their reassurance gave her hope. Although she could not stop her tears from falling constantly, she told herself in that brief moment that she would have to be patient.

As Ong waited, an uncle of hers who was also a pilot arrived at the airport. Other pilots followed suit. "When my

CHAPTER 1

uncle Moua Chue arrived, I was crying so he hugged me and had me sit down on a chair. Lee Teng came over. Vang Bee. All of the friends. Since Pao went down, they all came by. After a while, they all went into the office. It was only Moua Chue and I sitting there. Soon, he left as well. I had a watch on, so when I arrived at the airport, it was past 11:00 A.M. At that moment, I felt bad that I didn't bring anything for my husband to eat. It was close to noon and the others had gone to eat. I didn't bring anything, so what would he eat when he returned? It was then that I passed out. When I woke up, it was around 4:00 P.M. They had moved me to the medical exam room next to the office. Since I didn't have a shirt on, they had covered me with a blanket. When I woke up, the nurse next to me said, 'Sister, are you awake?' I looked at her and I didn't say anything. She asked me several more times before I could mutter, 'Yes, I'm awake.' Then suddenly I stood up and asked, 'Where's my husband?' She held me and guided me to sit back down. She told me to sit down and she'd go get someone to come and talk to me." The nurse disappeared for a few minutes. When she returned, Moua Chue followed behind.

Upon seeing Moua Chue, Ong sat up and asked, "Uncle Chue, where's Pao?" She recalled him responding, with tears in his eyes, "We've not heard anything from Pao. Just stay calm. As soon as we hear anything, we will let you know." When the Lao commander heard that Ong was awake, he also came over to speak to her. After trying to reassure her that they were doing everything they could to find him, he told her that he would take her home. She did not want to leave the airport. If there were any news about Pao, Ong thought, the leaders would hear about it first. But she felt powerless and complied. "When we arrived at the house, he came in and talked to my in-laws. He was crying as well. After that, he left. That night I cried all night. It rained so hard all night. I fixed his part of the bed, but he didn't return. I couldn't even take care of my child. He was with my mother-in-law even though I was still nursing him. I don't know what she fed him that night!" She knew other women whose husbands were shot down. They either were never found or, if located, returned in body bags. She had hoped that he would be alive. She wondered if he were cold. Did he have anything to eat? Was he afraid? Images of Pao flashed through her mind over and over again as she lay in bed. She does not remember how much time passed before she fell asleep.

2

Early Life and the Quest for Knowledge

Pao was born in the region called Xaho (Xaj Hob), south of Padong in northeastern Laos, during the Franco Vietminh War (1946–1953, also known as the First Indochina War). As was a common practice among the Hmong in Laos, his father, Chai Moua Yang (Caiv Muas Yaj) had several wives. With Sua Cha (Sua Tsab), he had Pao and a daughter. About his year of birth, Pao said, "Generally, we Hmong do not keep written records. My mother told me that I was born during rice harvest time, so I assume that I must have been born around November or so. But 1948 is probably pretty close. Maybe plus or minus a year."

Some of his fondest childhood memories were daily activities with the village children. They utilized whatever they could access in their environment to occupy themselves. He recalled, "The kids did not have much to do besides following our elders around and playing games. We actually did not go to school. At the time, we did not even know that it was available. The most popular game that the village boys played was topspin." Young boys and their fathers carved wood into cone-shaped pieces before tying a string around it. Winners were

CHAPTER 2

determined by how long the top would spin following its release. Another aspect of these competitions entailed knocking off a spinning top with their own top. Boys of his generation also played a game called "hitting firewood bundles" (*ntau tshua*). As he explained: "We would go gather wooden sticks and lean them against each other. We then tried to hit the pile of woods with a wooden stick and whichever ones you hit became yours. We Hmong children just played like that every day. Sometimes our clothes would be ripped from these adventures, but it was fun, and we always returned home with joy."

Subsistence farming was the primary way that his family and other villagers supported themselves. It had always been their way of life. Children gained skills from observing parents and other elders. Knowledge had been orally passed down from one generation to the next. Until recently, no written documents existed to record their life experiences or to instruct them on how to survive in the vast mountainous regions. Although literacy in their language is a more recent experience for Hmong, the value of writing had been an important part of their history where legends and myths refer to Hmong writing that had been suppressed by dominant forces.[1] As part of France's civilizing mission, school became available to the few who could afford it. Those who learned to read and write were given lower-level positions in the colonial administration; thus, literate individuals were revered by all. In the early 1950s, Western missionaries and linguists collaborated to develop a writing system for the Hmong language based on the Romanized Popular Alphabet.[2] This enabled many to learn how to read and write. Literacy in the Hmong language, however, was mainly for the purpose of communication within the Hmong population and conversion of Hmong to Christianity. In order to have access to opportunities outside of the villages, people had to learn the Lao language. French was also taught. The challenge for most Hmong at the time was the lack of schools in the remote areas where the vast majority lived.

28

EARLY LIFE AND THE QUEST FOR KNOWLEDGE

Pao's parents had heard about school being available in the larger towns, and they wanted him to be literate. He explained, "They didn't really know what school meant. [They'd] never seen it. Just heard people talk about it. That was just our way of life then!" His path to formal education seemed to be by chance when he was about eight. As he recounted, "In our part of [the] country, there was only Chaomeung [district chief] Youa Tong Yang's school at Khang Khay [in Xiengkhouang province]. Our village had no school. But one day, there were two Lao men who came to our village. They said they were literate, and they offered to teach the children. The parents agreed to hire them to teach the village children. Our parents paid each one of them one silver bar per year. They agreed to teach about ten of us. Like the Hmong saying, we learned like we were just wandering around for about a year. We learned basic reading and writing, just minimal. For example, we could read the words—so if the elders received a letter, we would read it—even though we did not understand what [the words] meant. When we read the letter out loud, the elders would then translate the words."

Soon after these first ten students started learning how to read and write, more parents wanted their children to participate. To demonstrate their support, they came together to help build a school. "They cut the logs into large parts. We Hmong call it ka tia [kab tiab] so it's smooth. That is how we initially had a board to write on. We had no papers. We just listened to the teachers and regurgitated what they said. No books to take home. We had one book for the whole class, only the teacher's book. We would just take turns reading from this book. We just tried to memorize. Whatever you can remember, that's it." The villagers soon bought a blackboard and chalk. This enabled the students to practice writing, which Pao believed positively enhanced their literacy skills. More importantly, however, this experience inspired Pao and other village children to seek ways to pursue formal education. The biggest barrier for them was that education in Xaho beyond the self-constructed village

CHAPTER 2

school was nonexistent. Toward the end of World War II, six tribal schools were founded for ethnic minority peoples. They were referred to as "mobile schools." Hmong living in the main towns in Xiengkhouang province could enroll in the schools.[3] The overall quality of education in Laos was quite problematic in terms of teacher experiences, school buildings, and materials.[4] Memorization and reciting of lessons was the standard assessment of learning outcomes. From the early 1950s through the early 1960s, formal education remained accessible to only a few wealthy families. That would gradually change with U.S. involvement.

Despite the enormous hardship and suffering that the Secret War brought to the people of Laos, it opened up new educational opportunities resulting from American financial backing. As the war in Vietnam escalated, the activities in the Long Cheng valley transformed into a "secret city" where CIA operatives, other intelligence officers, and humanitarian aides worked hand in hand to support the U.S.-sponsored war effort. When war came to Pao's family's village, they fled to Long Cheng. Without land to farm, Pao had to succumb to doing whatever was necessary to survive. He recalled this period as tumultuous, "At Long Cheng I found work with naikong [mini district chief] Nao Yeng Lee. He was in charge of overseeing the displaced people at Long Cheng. I went to help them by making coffee or babysitting. I was about fourteen. Old enough to know how to desire things. Old enough to know how to be embarrassed." In the village, Pao had no clue about the material things that existed in Long Cheng. Planes, jeeps, Western-style homes, and a wide range of food were enjoyed by the privileged who served the few Americans. The wealth they had amassed enabled some to establish restaurants, tailor shops, and convenience stores. Greater exposure increased his desire for these goods. He was, however, realistic about his financial situation.

As luck would have it, Pao's chance encounter with a male peer while the two were courting young women together

30

would open new doors that changed his life's direction forever. He remembered, "My parents were very poor, so I actually did not think about going to school at first. I did want to go to school because I saw my peers doing so, but I actually had no idea what to do. One day, I met Yee Her. He was from Khang Khay and was a nephew of Chaomeung [district chief] Youa Tong Yang. He and a friend were students in Vientiane. They had come back to visit Long Cheng to court the girls there. When I met them, Yee asked me if I'd be interested in going to school. I said, 'Yes, but where would I go?' He said, 'In Vientiane.' I told him I did not know anyone in Vientiane, so where would I live? He said that I could live with him." Pao could not believe what he had been offered. He was excited about the opportunity. "I ran home to tell my mom about it. She was supportive, but we both knew that we didn't have the money. With several wives, my father did not live with us. He had moved to another village so that he and the minor wife [*niam yau*] could farm." As typical of Hmong men with multiple wives, the minor wife was preferred. Sadly for Pao, the little that his father did make would go to support the minor wife and her children. He had a father, but the neglect, as he put it, made the situation similar to not having one at all.

A few days later, his mother told Pao that he should go to Vientiane with his friend. He was surprised at her insistence. She seemed to have understood how much he desired to pursue formal education and was willing to make the necessary sacrifices. "I remember clearly that she had only 5,000 kip [about $20] in her bag. That was her whole life's saving!"[5] With tears streaming down her face, she gave Pao 3,000 kip. He remembers the moment clearly. As he recounted the conversation with her, tears filled his eyes. He accepted her gift with determination to succeed. Unlike the children and relatives of military officers who had ongoing financial support, Pao knew that he would have to work harder and rely on the generosity of whomever he came across. With her blessing, he packed the few

CHAPTER 2

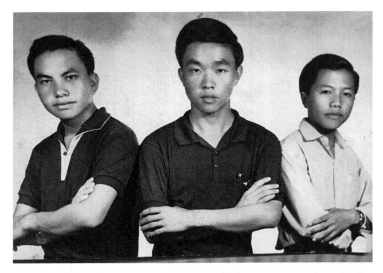

Yee Her (center) helped Pao (right) go to school in Vientiane. Circa 1963. (Pao Yang and Ena Yang collection)

belongings he had and followed Yee Her to Sam Thong, which was the American-sponsored humanitarian center, to wait for an airplane ride to Vientiane. That was because, in 1962, no big planes were available at the Long Cheng airstrip. After about a month's wait, they were finally able to get a ride to Vientiane. It would be Pao's first time on a plane. While he struggled to grapple with how such a heavy object could fly, he admitted that it was an exhilarating experience. He felt slightly sick as the helicopter descended. Fear did cross his mind. As they landed in Vientiane, he took a deep breath and embraced the fact that a new chapter in his quest for knowledge had begun.

Upon arrival in Vientiane, he lived in Chaomeung Youa Tong Yang's house with other young Hmong who had come to pursue their educational dreams. He enrolled in a public school called Chao Anou and started attending classes on August 15, 1962. It was across the street from Chaomeung Youa Tong's house and near what is today the Lao international soccer field.

*Pao (*back row, third from left*) made some new friends when he studied in Vientiane, 1963. (Pao Yang and Ena Yang collection)*

Since he did not have much money, Pao was relieved that he only had to walk across the street to go to school. But that was not the biggest challenge Pao faced. He was motivated, but his education by then had been only rudimentary. He also had limited access to learning materials. "As a poor kid, I had no other choice but to study hard. I had only two outfits, one notebook, and one pencil. Although I was older, I had to learn with little kids since I had to start at grade two. After two and a half months, it was demoralizing to have to learn along with small children, so I searched for a different school." Pao's ex-

CHAPTER 2

perience was not unusual. Most ethnic minorities did not have access to schools at a young age. Many started at an older age than ethnic Lao children who lived in major towns. Students moved to the next grade level after they had passed exams, so it was common to see classrooms with students of various ages. What was uncomfortable for Pao was that the age gap between him and the elementary students was wide. He was already a young man. Sitting in a classroom with small children made him feel inadequate, especially when their performances exceeded his own.

When he enrolled at Xi Than Tai (Xim Thaa Taib) school, he asked to be placed in a higher grade because of his age. The school leaders agreed. Even though he was behind the students in his age group, it was less embarrassing. The instruction was conducted in Lao and French. His Lao language skill was basic, and he was learning French for the first time. Even though the French had officially left Laos in 1955, the Royal Lao Government kept in place the educational system the French had developed. In addition, French missionaries continued to operate schools in Laos and the French government provided scholarships for children of the Lao elite to study in France for years after French colonial rule ended.[6] Pao studied extremely hard during the school year. He lost sleep trying to catch up. At Xi Than Tai, an exam was administered at the end of each school year to determine who could go to Dong Dok (teacher training college). Despite his best efforts, he was not adequately prepared. He failed the exam that would have been his ticket to what he thought would be a better life. Pao ran out of money, and the generosity of his friends ceased as well. For several days after the exam results, he lost sleep over the thought of returning to Long Cheng as a failure. His mother would continue to help him, but he knew that he could not depend on her for too much longer since she could barely support herself and his younger sister. It was imperative that he find a solution himself.

*Pao (*far left, with cap*) enjoying a picnic with friends at Phou Khao Khouay area. Circa 1966. (Pao Yang and Ena Yang collection)*

Being in Vientiane had exposed him to other opportunities. He had learned about French and American Catholic missionaries helping other young Hmong attend school that included room and board. Although not a convert, Pao took a chance in asking them for help. He was thrilled that they took him in. "I went to live with Father Nhia Pao [Txiv plig Nyiaj Pov, whose French name is Father Yves Bertrais]. There were four priests: Father Nhia Pao, Father Neng Va, Father Shong Leng, Father Vang Xu. Father Vang Xu was American. All the others were French. Living with the priests was cheaper. Each month I paid only 600 kip [$2.50], but food was included."

Catholic-sponsored schools were considered to be higher quality than those operated by the Lao government. Pao continued to struggle academically, but the challenging environment also forced him to work harder so that he would make significant progress. "There were French teachers. I attended the school for a year with fifty-two students. When we tested, I

CHAPTER 2

placed at thirty-two because my education level was quite low. I was older, so again it was embarrassing, but I knew that it was all I could do. I just had to continue to work hard. This paid off because at the end of the second year, I passed the exam, so I was able to catch up to my friends who had passed the year before. I was placed in level A, and not long after that, I was able to enter the teacher training institute in the Dong Dok area. If you entered this school, you would receive [a] full scholarship from the government. You didn't have to pay tuition, but when you finished, you had to be either a teacher or a soldier. It was good for my mother when I entered Dong Dok. She finally did not have to support me anymore."

This was a proud moment for Pao. He had dreamed about it, but it did take a few days for it to sink in. His hard work and his mother's investment in him finally paid off. Regarding his father, who spent all of his time with the minor wife, Pao declared, "It's sad that I didn't have a father to share the joys in my life with. I had a father, but he lived with his second wife and her children, so it was mostly my mother and me." Whereas some men actively supported multiple wives, others neglected the first wives once they married minor wives. Wealthy men could continue to provide food and shelter, but for men with modest means, the first wives and their children often are left to fend for themselves. Consequently, Pao's heartache was common.

In Vientiane and away from the war zone, Pao could focus on his studies, but when he managed to return to Long Cheng, he confronted the reality of a growing war. He had returned to visit his family in August 1968. While hanging out with some other young men, he heard a Lao Laum Phao [United Lao Race] radio announcement that the military was recruiting people to be trained as pilots. He recalled being intrigued about it, but he was aware that the military was plagued with factionalism and nepotism. When there were positions, they were often given not based on merit but on social relations. He thought about it more seriously and realized that if he were to have any chance of being selected, he needed to have a plan. "Often, if you are not related to the leaders, no matter how educated or smart you may be, you would not get to go. They would choose someone from their family first because of the financial benefits. So, I went to Colonel Shoua Yang, who's an uncle from our Yang clan. I told him that I was interested, so he asked me how much education I had. After I told him about my education background, he said, 'If you are serious about it, then I'll take you. Get in the car.' So, he drove me down to General Vang Pao's house. He told Colonel Moua Gao to put my name on the list. After a few days, I was called to go train." Pao's experience is similar to how most of the other trainees were selected. A basic requirement was that they be literate. The level of education was subjectively determined by military officers who either knew the young men themselves or their fellow officers recommended certain individuals to them. Power and prestige from high CIA payments was the primary reason why high-ranking officers often chose those related to them. When casualty among pilots became a grave concern, wealthy families chose to not allow their sons to participate in aviation training, which opened up opportunities for individuals like Pao.

Pao was motivated to embark on this dangerous path for two reasons. "First, I knew that I was an only son. I knew that throughout history, there had not been Hmong pilots. So, I wanted to see if I could be one. The second reason was that I thought that if I could be a pilot, I would be able to help my people." Pao was enthusiastic about being selected because he thought that he could make a difference for his ethnic group. Thinking back to the moment he found out that he had been chosen, Pao admitted that he feared breaking the news to his mother the most. When he told her his plans, she vehemently disagreed with his decision. She pointed out the tragic outcomes for the pilots who came before him and reminded him of the fact that he was her only son. What would she do if something terrible happened to him? There were so many other

CHAPTER 2

young men who wished to become pilots. Why did the leaders not choose someone from a family with multiple sons? She shouted out more reasons for why Pao should not go, but she soon realized that it was useless to try to influence his decision. It was not up to her. He had made up his mind.

3

To Fly the Iron Eagle

Hmong referred to airplanes as iron eagles (dav hlau/dlaav hlau). When American military personnel first came to recruit them, the locals were in awe at the sight of an aircraft. As U.S. involvement in Laos increased, Air America planes, especially as they dropped food on mountainsides, became a common sight for villagers. If they lived in locations with an airstrip—also referred to as lima sites—such as Long Cheng and Sam Thong, they could catch a ride with one of the transport aircraft to other locations. This subsequently reduced the local population's fear of airplanes.

Though a dangerous job, pilots were paid well. This was because Hmong T-28 pilots, in particular, were paid by both the RLA and the CIA. Their salaries brought great wealth to their families. Cov tub tsav dav hlaus (the sons flying iron eagles) were revered by the young and old. Thus, being selected for training was great news for Pao. Not only would he soon be able to learn how to fly an iron eagle, but he also looked forward to the financial benefits. Pao was part of the third group of Hmong pilot trainees to go to Thailand. Since American and

CHAPTER 3

Lao leaders initially resisted allowing Hmong to participate, the first two Hmong T-28 pilots, Lue Lee and Toua Vang, did not go through the Royal Lao Air Force process. Instead, General Vang Pao and CIA operatives pulled strings to have them trained as fighter pilots. Lue was a teacher, and Toua had studied in France. With formal education, they were believed to be more likely to succeed, which would help to demonstrate that Hmong could fly. Toua's aircraft disappeared shortly after he received his wings, and it was never found. Lue, on the other hand, would go on to become an ace pilot, flying about five thousand missions. His aircraft was shot down in July 1969. He and Neng Lo, a new graduate who was sitting in the rear of his aircraft, both died. Lue Lee continues to be a legendary pilot for the Hmong people, and Americans who worked with him describe him as a hero who made the ultimate sacrifice.

By the time Pao's group was in training, Lao military leaders argued that Military Region II pilot trainees should go through the same process as other Royal Lao pilots since they would eventually be working together. Though enthusiastic about having been selected, Pao realized that he was once again ill-prepared. He was proficient in French, but since he had studied English for only about two hours a week at Dong Dok, his English language skills were not enough. He had not studied English seriously because, like his peers, he did not think there would be any need for it in Laos. He thought to himself that, again, he would have to work very hard to overcome any barriers in his way.

Pao believes that ethnic animosity contributed to what happened to his group. After they had completed ground school in Udorn and Khon Khaen, Thailand, and received their private pilot licenses, the group members were sent back to Vientiane. "The Lao people in charge said that they weren't sure we understood English, so they wouldn't let us enter the T-28 pilot training program. In Vientiane, we were sent to learn English at Phone Kheng military center. After about eight months of English language classes, they assessed our skills. We all passed, so we were all ready to go to training, but they still wouldn't let us go. They said we had to go to Savannakhet [in southern Laos] so that they can test our flying skills. Those leaders did everything they could to try and prove that we should not be allowed to be [fighter] pilots. So, we went to Savannakhet. We flew the planes with one Lao pilot in the back. It was only after we proved that we could operate a plane that we were allowed to return to Thailand to participate in T-28 training." Pao suggests that the roundabout process he and his fellow trainees were forced to follow was the result of Lao prejudice toward ethnic minorities like the Hmong.

When the group returned to Thailand, the Thai instructors said that the Hmong names were too difficult for them to pronounce, but the real issue was that they did not want the general public to know about the Hmong pilot trainees. Instructors gave each man a Thai first name. Pao's was Saleunphoon. On paper, the Thai name was listed next to the Hmong name. When interacting with instructors, other staff on site, and the public, they used their Thai names. However, on official paperwork that American military officials provided, such as certificates, their Hmong names were used. His cohort consisted of eleven Hmong and one Kmhmu. One of the initial steps in their training process was the physical exam, which not everyone passed. Once the exams were completed, only ten moved on to the next stage. Six months into the training, two people, Ying Lee and Ge Lo, were sent to train as mechanics at Hua Hin, Thailand. Pao recounts, "They were both very good academically, but when it came to operating an aircraft, they just couldn't do it."

The thrill of learning to fly slowly dissipated as Pao fully immersed himself in training. "I didn't know exactly what pilot training would entail. I thought that we would be flying

CHAPTER 3

the small porter planes that provided transportation to people. It was only when you started training that you realized what you had to do." After they were selected for training, it was not a guarantee that they would become fighter pilots. "For my group, we all did not think we would be learning to fly fighter airplanes. In fact, we learned to fly the C-47 (Dakota) and helicopters. When we finished, we were told by General Vang Pao to go back and learn to become fighter pilots because the pilots before us had died. We had no choice but to go back accordingly." Pao was afraid and thinks that other trainees were as well, but they did not talk about their feelings. Everyone was trying to not wash out.

Training for Pao consisted of many ups and downs. At times, he doubted himself. "In the morning, we learned about what flying involved. In the evening, we learned English. It was called ground school, where we were taught facts about the planes. What makes a plane able to fly, weather conditions, flight regulations, et cetera. It's not as if you showed up and then just learned to fly the plane. There were certainly many procedures that we had to learn. When we were learning how to fly small planes, the instructors were Thai. There are two kinds: Cessna 150 and 180. They brought those planes to be used at Long Cheng later on during the war. When we first learned to fly, we actually flew what they called Piper Cub. It was a training plane by Thai instructors. But when we trained to be fighter pilots, it was American instructors. However, there was one Lao commander who was sent to help oversee and train those of us from Laos. So, some of us had the Lao instructor. By the time our group was training to be T-28 pilots, there were only seven of us left. My instructor's name was Thompson, Captain Thompson, but I do not know his full name. Of course, at that time I never thought about keeping in touch with him because I never imagined that I would someday be in this country." A couple of former Hmong pilots have reconnected with their American instructors in the United States,

42

but the vast majority were similar to Pao. The American instructors were young men at the time who did one or two tours in Southeast Asia and then moved on to other opportunities. Most also did not keep track of the students with whom they worked during the war.

Ground school and flight training were stressful to Pao and the other students, but it was also an exciting time because they became exposed to a whole new way of life. At Udorn, they attended ground school during the week, and they partied hard on weekends. Most American IPs did not socialize with students from Laos. The few who did went along with Thai IPs. Visits to bars and brothels were common activities. The place they visited most frequently was Savanh Vieng Pheng, where forty to fifty prostitutes stood behind windows. Once a customer decided on a woman, he would go around to the counter and present the woman's number to the host. Soon thereafter, he would be led to the room with the woman he had chosen. In addition, Thai instructors held drinking parties where they hired dancers to entertain the trainees. Party halls and nude dancers were rented, and there were plenty of drinks to go around. The men danced and drank until they were about to pass out, as Pao put it. But he remembers that a chauffeur stood by to take them back to the rental house.

Pao remembers being in the midst of some horrifying incidents. "Some IPs took us to bars and treat[ed] us to meals and girls. They had more money than us. We often went in groups and to various locations because people preferred different establishments. I remember one IP, who was a huge American, getting robbed. He was drunk and walking around. Thieves held a knife to his side, and so he had no choice but to hand over his thick wallet." Because of the pilots' newfound wealth, young Thai women often pursued them. Some of the Hmong trainees did marry Thai women, but Pao stated that these were not the women they met at bars. He explained, "The women that some of our pilots married were not prostitutes. They were

CHAPTER 3

Pao attended T-28D Koua Xiong's marriage to Chanhpheng. (Pao Yang and Ena Yang collection)

women who were hired to cook and clean for us." His fellow trainee Koua Xiong met his wife differently. Pao continued, "Koua liked to smoke a lot so he would go walk around while having a cigarette. One day he stopped by a shop to buy cigarettes and met a girl who had come from the country to stay with her sister and help her with the shop. He talked to her and when he returned, he told me that he met a girl he liked very much." After this encounter, Pao would go with him to talk to the girl whenever they had free time. Not long after, she invited the two of them to visit her parents in the country. After they graduated and had returned to Laos, Koua decided to return to marry this girl and Pao accompanied him to serve as the best man.

Despite the fact that they were captivated by life in Thailand, the Hmong pilot trainees knew their fate. As visitors with a mission to earn their wings and return to the battlefield, they were aware that their stay would be temporary. Flight training that usually would require several years was shortened to less than a year. IPs and students alike struggled to effectively communicate with each other. In some cases, this stalled the progress that they needed to make. Pao admitted that it was a miracle that he graduated because he experienced so many difficulties. He remembers the first time he flew solo as frightening. "That's because every day before that you sat in the front and operated the plane but your instructor was in the back, so you were reassured that even in life-threatening situations you still had your instructor to save you. On the day that I was going to fly solo, all of the other six Hmong trainees also were scheduled to go solo. There was a total of twenty pilots training at the time. Seven of us were Hmong and all were going solo. Only one Lao pilot got to go solo that same day. Just before it was my time to fly solo, I took off twice with my instructor. When we landed the second time, he told me to taxi my plane back to the parking area. When we reached the parking lot, he told me to not turn off the engine yet." Pao had not expected to fly solo, so he was not sure why his IP told him to do that. However, he did as instructed.

Pao kept the engine running and watched as his IP carried his parachute and got out of the aircraft. As he waited, he thought that maybe he had done something wrong and the IP was going to explain to him as he had done many times. When the IP did not speak, Pao asked him what was going on. "He responded, 'You're on your own. This time I'm not going with you. You'll have to go by yourself. Dead or alive I'm not going to be with you.' At this moment, my entire body began to shiver, and I didn't know where to start because the instructor was not going to be there to tell me what to do. It was exciting, but fear overtook me because I was afraid that after I took off, I wouldn't be able to land or that I would make a mistake. It was a scary moment. But my instructor said, 'You're going alone now. Go for about an hour and then come back. Once you're in the air, you can do whatever you like. Just do what I taught you. I'll have a radio and I'll call you.' So that was it.

CHAPTER 3

I was on my own, but I didn't go for an hour because it was scary. I came back after about twenty, thirty minutes. When I landed, he shook my hand and congratulated me. He had already called the mechanics at the Udorn base to tell them to prepare a bucket of water because today his student was going solo. They were instructed to let me remove my paperwork from my pockets and then pour water over me. It was an exciting moment!" IPs determined when a student was ready to fly solo. Some students were more confident than others, so when informed that they were going to be allowed to go solo, they were ecstatic. Pao admitted that he was not one of them. He questioned his own abilities despite the fact that his IP thought he had been adequately prepared.

Reaching this point was not a smooth path. In fact, Pao witnessed frustration from fellow trainees and IPs. That was because flying a plane requires good health overall. "It's not like learning to read and write, where if you have good memory, you will do well. It's different from going to school. Also, you can be a strong athlete, but if you are in the air and the plane rolls a couple times, you may [get nauseated], throw up, or black out. If this happens, then an instructor would say that the person could not continue to learn to fly. If he continued, he would likely die. That's why there were some who were very good students. I could never beat them at that. But when it came to flying [airplanes], they did not do well. Some had excessive headaches as the plane ascended. Others were colorblind." Many experienced extreme motion sickness, but most were able to overcome it not long after they began training. In some cases, IPs purposely flipped aircraft over and over again and laughed excessively as students became sick. This angered the students and made them want to quit altogether. The students learned afterward that the IPs did so to determine if the students could fly. If they were not able to overcome motion sickness, then there was no need for them to remain in the program.

46

Pao's T-28 training certificate signed by USAF officer. (Pao Yang and Ena Yang collection)

What Pao found most difficult to bear was how some IPs treated students. "The instructors yelled at us frequently. If they could hit us, I think they would have done so. Some of the instructors were cruel. If you messed up, they would grab the control and roll the plane abruptly so that you didn't even have time to prepare yourself. They were quite evil. There were times when I wondered if I would be able to finish. Many times, I doubted myself and I thought about quitting and returning home for good. This was especially true when the instructors yelled at us. They said terrible things, like *shit*. But the truth is that what hurt the most was when it came from the Lao instructors because we understood everything they said. Because we didn't understand all of what the American instructors said, it didn't hurt as much. The Americans' behaviors were very different. No matter what happened in the air and how much they yelled at you, once you landed, they patted you on

CHAPTER 3

the back and said sorry and shook your hand. The Lao instructors wouldn't even look at you. They would just grab their parachute and go straight to the debriefing room." Crushed and humiliated, some trainees did not even share their struggles with fellow trainees. They swallowed their pride and hoped for a better experience the next day.

4

Love and War

While still in pilot training, Pao was presented with a proposition. In 1970, Pao's uncle Youa Chong Yang (Ntsuab Txoov Yaj), sent him a photo of a thirteen-year-old girl. Youa Chong informed Pao that he liked the girl and was considering marrying her; however, Pao's mother told him that she had met this girl and knew her parents. The girl's beauty was captivating, and his mother suggested to his uncle that he ask Pao to see if he would like to marry her first. If Pao was not interested, then Youa Chong could go ahead and ask for her hand in marriage. After receiving the photo, Pao returned to Long Cheng as soon as he had a free weekend. He wasted no time once back in Long Cheng. As customary in arranged marriages, he sought male elders from his clan to assist him in asking for her parents' permission to marry her. Once he had found the necessary negotiators, the group headed toward Ong's parents' village, Phouvieng.

Ong revealed, "The honest truth is that we did not know each other at all!" In fact, she said that she did not remember ever meeting him before the day he showed up with elders to

CHAPTER 4

Pao (right) and his uncle Youa Chong Yang were close friends who looked out for each other. (Pao Yang and Ena Yang collection)

request for her hand in marriage. However, their families were related. "My mother is one of his aunts. Pheng's [Ong and Pao's son] grandmother [Pao's mother] is one of my father's cousins. We lived in the same region, so they knew each other. We were at Pha Khao, but because of the war, we moved to Phouvieng and Pao's family moved to Long Cheng. The families were separated so we didn't know each other." Hmong have traditionally preferred to intermarry with people who are close relatives. Cross-cousin marriages were thought to be ideal arrangements since they are assumed to further strengthen family relations. Some believe that such unions have a higher probability of succeeding since both sides are invested in maintaining strong kinship ties. In instances where the marriages fail, family relations can be severed. Consequently, some families do caution against cross-cousin marriages for fear of strained social relations if divorce or separation occurs.

Because of what happened after he was shot down, Pao chose to speak very little of his marriage to Ong during the several interviews. When he did not return after the war ended, his relatives pressured Ong to marry one of his relatives. Instead, she chose to marry someone outside of his clan. Each had remarried before they could be reunited. This complicated situation resulted in Pao offering only brief comments with few details whenever Ong came up in conversations. It is possible that he held back feelings about her because the interviews I conducted with him were in his home. Although his second wife went on with other household chores during the interviews, she was present. His expressions suggested that it may have been painful to dwell on this part of his past.

Ong has no recollection of ever meeting him before he came to ask her parents' permission to marry her. She spoke at length about how she and Pao ended up marrying each other. It was after they were already married that Pao told Ong he had previously seen her. She recounted, "As a young girl, I had followed my elders to Long Cheng many times. [Pao's] grandmother is a great-aunt, but since we didn't live together, I didn't know her. One time, she saw me and she said, 'Young lady, whose daughter are you? You are so lovely!' I told her, 'I'm my father's daughter.' She asked, 'Who is your father and why are you so lovely?' I told her, 'My father is Xai Her.' She asked, 'Is he my cousin [dab laug] Xai Her?' I told her that I didn't know. 'Where do you live?' she asked. I told her that we

CHAPTER 4

lived in Phouvieng, Hai Hong [Haib Hoob]. She exclaimed, 'In that case, it is my cousin Xai Her!' She pulled me toward her and hugged me. I was just a young girl, so she held me in her arms. Then, she left." The purpose of that trip was to buy fabric and other materials to prepare for the approaching New Year celebration. Once they returned to their village, Ong's mother worked diligently to sew a new costume for her to wear. For young girls like Ong, this was an exciting time of the year. Despite the war taking place, they looked forward to showing off their new clothes, which was a sign of wealth. Young men traveled from one village to another looking for eligible young women to court.

After the New Year festivities, most villagers returned to the fields to farm, if they lived in areas where they could farm. What they cultivated was mostly for consumption, but many did try to sell their crops in order to have money to buy things that they could not produce themselves. Ong's mother was motivated to earn money, so one day, she decided to gather a bunch of sugar cane stalks and bananas to sell at the Long Cheng market. That was because women, children, and the elderly lived among soldiers. Its inhabitants had limited access to land to garden. As a result, people from nearby villages brought their produce to sell at the market. When Ong asked her mother if she could accompany her, her mother agreed.

When they arrived at the market, her mother spread out the sugar canes and bananas on a stall. She had hoped that people would buy everything soon so that they could return home. Ong remembers that the market was lively. Many like her mother were merely trying to survive with the little money that they made, but other vendors were wealthy entrepreneurs. It was not just selling fruits and vegetables. Some operated noodle soup and tailor shops. Military officers who had unlimited access to CIA aircraft brought back a wide range of products from Vientiane to sell to the local residents. If frequent takeoff and landing of T-28D aircraft and helicopters were not taking place, Ong said that life almost seemed normal.

Pao's uncle Youa Chong had recently returned to Long Cheng. He was a young man (*tias hluas ntsaug*). People like him would go to the market to scout out girls helping their parents. Ong remembers the incident clearly, "My mother and I were waiting at the market when he approached us. He was all by himself. I remember him saying, 'Hello, Aunt, where are you from?' My mother responded, 'We are from Phouvieng, Ha Hong.' He asked, 'Are those sugar canes, Na Va (Naj Vam) sugar canes?' My mother responded that it was Na Va sugar canes. He bought two sugar cane stalks and a cluster of bananas. He then left us for a while." Ong had no clue where he went, but when he returned, he did not have the items with him.

As typical of Hmong social practices, young men generally do not directly engage in conversations with young women in front of their parents. They would speak to the parents first. Youa Chong continued conversing with Ong's mother almost as though he had not left them at all. "He asked, 'How old is your daughter?' My mother responded to him, 'Oh, we just count one harvest from one field after another. We don't know anything about age!' So, he stopped asking her questions, but he wouldn't leave us alone. He kept hanging around near me. I could sense that he was trying to befriend me. At the time, my uncle [mother's brother] had passed away and there was only my aunt left. My mother told me to go to my aunt's house to see if breakfast is ready so that we could go eat with them." Ong took off in the direction of her aunt's house. She walked fast and lost sight of the man who attempted to follow her. "But as I approached the road that curved toward the airstrip, I saw him following me. When he reached me, he asked, 'Hey young lady, where are you going?' He continued, 'Could I accompany you?' I was so frightened! I didn't know what to do. I thought that if I yelled at him, it might offend him. If I didn't, I might be in

CHAPTER 4

danger. At that time, there were many Thai soldiers around. I thought to myself that if I went alone, I may run into them. So, he went with me. But I didn't know how to talk to him. He just followed me. When we reached the houses, he asked me into whose house I was going to go. I pointed to the house and then I went inside. He left and I had no idea what he did after." Not long after this encounter, Pao came to ask Ong's parents to marry her. Older men marrying significantly younger women was common. Young women had very little say in the process. Pao was much older, but at the time, she did not know how much older he was. It was after they were already married that his father told Ong that Pao was twenty-three when he married her. Since she was only about fourteen, Pao did seem so much older to her. She confessed that she found it hard to love him at first due to the age difference.

At the beginning of their marriage, Ong would tell him how much she despised him whenever she was angry. One day, he declared that he understood her behavior because he had seen her before they married. "I told him I hated him, and he said that I had always been mad at him. I asked him how that was possible. He told me that when his village was moving away from the battlefield, they had stayed at Ba Cher [Bam Cawb] near Xaho [Xaj Hob]. They had set up camp near Nou Chong Mountain [Tsua Noo Tsoov] near Aunt Choua Ying [Phauj Txoo Yeeb]. 'We came to farm near Na Va, near your village,' he said. 'At the time I was already a young man, and I was already interested in courting girls and going hunting. You wore a long shirt. You were talkative. When my mother and I came to your house, you had some chicken in your name [elders like to do that to children—allocate domesticate animals to their children]. Your mother gave my mother a beautiful hen to take with us since we had lost everything when we moved. The following morning when you woke up, your mother told you that she had given us your hen. You cursed

54

that I was an evil Hmong person who had come to steal your hen. You took a stick and pushed it into the fire pit with smoke and ashes flying everywhere.' He continued, 'I actually didn't want to take the hen, but since your mother insisted, I took it. You cried about the ordeal, so, yes, you had always been angry with me.'" Ong has no memory of the event, but she said it could have happened since she loved to help her parents look after the chicken.

When she reflects about her marriage to Pao, Ong describes it as a dream. Immediately after the wedding, Pao had to go back to Thailand to complete pilot training. He left Ong to live with his mother. She jokingly remarked that she spent more time with his mother than with him. During the nearly two years that they were married, she did grow to love him. After he finished training and returned to Long Cheng, they were apart during the day, but he would return home after work. "My love for him grew because he was my husband, especially after I had Pheng. I would look at my son and then my husband and it made me love my husband so much." Each morning she helped him get dressed before he went to work. "Once he's dressed, I'd touch his clothes. If I didn't hug him, he'd asked, 'Aren't you going to hug me?' At the time, I was so young and when I looked at him, he seemed so tall. I'd stand on his shoes in order for my face to reach his. Then I'd hug him. He would tell me that he'd return soon. I couldn't ask him anything. All I could say was, 'Will you be back for lunch?' He'd usually say, 'I won't return. I'll eat at the airport, and I'll be back in the evening.' My heart ached and I'd ask him how many missions he [would] go [on]. His response was that he would go on two missions but that he wasn't sure if he'd have to fill in for anyone. I'd beg him to fly only his missions, and he'd say OK. He knew how much I worried. As soon as he parked his motorbike outside, tears would fall down my face. I'd rush out and touch him. I'd rub his back, head, and face. I don't know if he thought

CHAPTER 4

Ong, Pao, and Pheng, 1971. (Photo courtesy Ong Moua)

I was afraid for him or that I missed him. He'd put his arms around me and we'd go inside. When he saw my tears, he'd say, 'You can see me off, then come and wait for me to return every day.' I told him that would be great."

Pao and Ong followed a daily routine. Before he went to work, Pao would drop Ong off at the morning market. Ong asserted these were some of her happiest days. "I'd go buy vegetables, then return home by taxi, cook for the elders, clean the house, and take care of my child. He would be done around 4:00 P.M. I'd walk to wait for him at the location he indicated. It was in front of a store near That Luang [Buddhist stupa] that sold flip flops. I'd watch for him as motorbikes passed by. He knew I would be waiting there, so when he arrived, he'd stop, and I'd hop on. We did this every day until the day he was shot down." Ong tried to fight back tears as she narrated the dreadful day that she referred to as the reason for her experiencing a lifetime of grief and sorrow. The heartache that is associated with this part of her past remains. She could not prevent tears from falling excessively. Although decades have passed, she spoke as though she were still waiting for him to return to pick her up from the market.

5

No Room for Mistakes

Pao had seen how pilots went on missions and were killed in action from either being shot down by enemy guns or crashing due to aircraft malfunction or freak weather conditions. He knew what was expected of him once he accepted the offer to join the T-28 pilot training program. This responsibility was further reinforced when he succeeded in becoming a fighter pilot. "As soon as we finished and received our wings, we returned and were put to work. Half of the people who received wings were Americans and some were Lao. The Americans were not going to Laos with us, so they told us that because we would be fighter pilots, we must be careful. If we are not, then we could die." IPs reminded the new pilots that they would no longer accompany them. Whether the students lived or died was in their own hands, so they had to do their best to avoid antiaircraft missiles. Whereas ethnic Lao pilots had the option of being sent to all five regions, Hmong pilots had no choice. Pao explained, "For the Hmong pilots, they separated us. They knew that Vang Pao would not let us go serve anywhere else. So, they told us to go back to Long Cheng. We

CHAPTER 5

stopped in Vientiane en route to Long Cheng. They passed out uniforms and guns to us. It was at this moment that I realized it was no longer training, but war." After receiving their uniforms and guns, Pao's group proceeded to meet with the only two Hmong T-28 pilots left in Military Region II, Commander (deceased) Yang Xiong and Captain (KIA) Vang Sue. The others had all died. Pao recalled that the two men expressed much joy when they saw Pao's group, but soon their solemn looks overwhelmed the new pilots. That was because everyone knew the likely outcome for all. Pao revealed, "Verbally you didn't say anything, but inside, your heart is crying."

In addition to the heavy fighting in Military Region II, the runway at Long Cheng airport was exceptionally dangerous. It was located in the valley, with steep hills in the back and high mountains in the front. Pao recounted, "If you don't land accurately, then you will die. It's the same for takeoff. If you come in from the back, you do not accurately calculate, and you land closer to the end of the landing strip, you won't have enough time to hit the brake. You'd hit the mountains, and death is inevitable. If you have too many bombs and it's too heavy, it would affect your takeoff, and you could crash into the hills." There was no room for mistakes. They had trained in an area in Thailand with few nearby mountains, and they did not have to worry about the leveled airstrip in Udorn. Even though the new pilots had all received their wings, their skill levels varied. Most did not have to practice with the experienced pilots, but as a new pilot, Pao was afraid. He practiced a couple of times with Yang Xiong and Vang Sue sitting in the back to make sure he could take off and land safely. Once he was able to do so, then he was allowed to fly alone. The anxiety that he felt decreased after practicing a few more times, but he admitted that each takeoff and landing was as overwhelming as the first time he flew solo during training.

In addition to a short airstrip in a valley surrounded by vast mountains, the pilots regularly experienced equipment failure.

NO ROOM FOR MISTAKES

Pao was not able to drop bombs from his aircraft twice. If this occurred, then pilots were not allowed to land with the bombs at the Long Cheng airstrip. "You did not have a way to find out the real problem. When you attempt to drop the bombs and if you couldn't, the rules were that you were supposed to do all that you could to drop the bombs over thick jungles. You had to shake the aircraft. My bombs didn't release twice, so I had to try to land with them. I couldn't land with the bombs at Long Cheng because of the short airstrip. It was too dangerous! When this happened, then we had to go Vientiane to land because you need a longer airstrip to land with the bombs. The way it worked was that if your bombs couldn't be dropped, you could not land first. You had to let the other pilots land and you land last. You had to approach the landing strip very fast but also very low and you must not bounce because if you do, the bombs might drop and explode. So, the idea was that if you came last and your bombs exploded, it would affect only you because your friends have already landed, and you will be the only casualty. We also had problems with the rockets. With bombs, when you press the button, they would go down. The rockets are like bullets from a gun. Once pressed, they go forward and explode. When they do not explode, then you'd have to let your fellow pilots land after you because if they went ahead of you and you land behind them, the rockets might release and explode when you touch down and hit them. These were the procedures for fighter pilots. So many worries every mission!" Bomb and rocket failures were deadly situations if they occurred while pilots were in fast pursuit of enemies. This was especially true when they were charged to fly low to increase target accuracy. If a pilot dove in to drop a bomb over antiaircraft artillery but the bomb could not be released, it usually had a disastrous ending.

Pao continued about equipment problems, "The planes had [an] automatic parachute that [would] eject the pilot. But if you land and your door is open and you hit the parachute button,

CHAPTER 5

it will just strangle you. If you know that you can't land and decide that you're going to hit the parachute button, then you have to close the door. The door must be fully closed. Then, when you hit the button, you can be properly ejected, and you would not die." Death was a common scene in Long Cheng, however. Body bags were flown in throughout the day. It had become the norm to hear people keening as their loved ones were dropped off. Dying seemed so ordinary. Pao hoped that he would avoid it each time that he went on a mission.

Pao vividly remembers his first bombing mission. He said that things were complicated during the war, so pilots did not discuss their feelings. He did not know how his fellow pilots felt. As young men, they did not want to let others know that they were afraid. Each put forth a fearless performance, but inside, Pao reiterated, he was afraid. "The biggest fear was when I was nearing my target. That moment you just did not know which direction antiaircraft guns would shoot from. It was only after you dropped your bombs and you heard explosions that you [could] breathe. That first mission was indeed exceptionally scary. The enemies feared you, but you also feared them!" It seemed that more experience would make the missions easier, but Pao said that was not the case. The thick jungle and large caves enabled enemy forces to hide. What pilots confronted was the unpredictability of enemy responses to aircraft hovering over them. Ground soldiers at least could use the jungle and caves as cover, but the T-28Ds were in the open for the enemy to shoot at.

Since T-28Ds flew very low, they could not avoid a wide range of enemy guns. Pao added, "My plane was hit many times, but the good thing was that they were just small guns, like AK [47], so not too bad. Though [they were] small guns of course you were still scared, but what can you do?" Before each of the close to one thousand missions Pao completed, he went through the same thought process. "While you did not say anything, your mind wondered if you [would] be lucky this time. You asked yourself, 'What if I get shot down? What will

T-28D aircraft during training in Thailand, 1973. (Photo by Lieutenant Colonel [Retired] John Gunn)

happen to me?' This was always on your mind. You may smile on the outside, but deep inside, you could not smile. There was not much you could do about it. You had to do your job because people are depending on you." Often ground troops would be trapped between enemy forces so the pilots were their only hope of escaping. This increased the pressure on pilots even more. Not only did they have to be accurate in bombing the enemy, but they also had to avoid hitting their own men. One of Pao's greatest fears was that the explosions would be responsible for killing fellow soldiers.

Even though Pao was perpetually conflicted, following orders was the only option. "For the pilots, we did not do according to what we thought. We just followed directions from the government and military leaders. If they tell us to bomb a certain target, we did it. We often did not know who was below. Whether it was our own people, the enemy, or just people they disliked. If the leaders gave us the order, we just bombed

CHAPTER 5

them. We followed orders, and we often did not see what was on the ground. The leaders just ordered the T-28 pilots to drop bombs on military camps in these areas. The pilots did it simply because they were ordered to do so." Pao's revelation explains why he was persistently emotionally at odds with orders from his superiors. He followed them as instructed but he was not certain that collateral damage was not inflicted on friendly forces and civilians. Once bombs were dropped or rockets were fired, pilots fled from the target area. As a result, they never saw the extent of the damage they caused on the ground. Official reports documented the number of enemy soldiers killed and weapons destroyed. Causes for friendly combatant casualties and/or civilian deaths were only attributed to enemy fire. Pilots were aware of this problematic condition, but it was not their place to question their superiors.

While Pao carried out bombing missions as ordered, his loved ones could not concentrate on anything until they knew that he had safely returned to base. "My parents and wife often could not sit still. They wondered if I would come back. At that time, my mother loved me so much. Each day she would burn incense and place them on the altar outside of the house to ask for the ancestors' spirits to watch over me and to make sure I returned. Each day when I took off, my family was not motivated to do anything. No smiles on their faces. My mother could not even sew. She just sat at the doorstep waiting to see if her son would return. When I did return, then my family could smile again." Ong added, "I was extremely afraid! I worried about him excessively, but I never told him. I never talked about it to the elders. I kept it all inside. The elders said not to ask any questions. No harsh words. You can't tell him not to go in front of them." Thousand-year-old beliefs warn Hmong about the danger of openly discussing their innermost feelings with anyone. She had been taught that if evil spirits heard family members express fear for Pao, they may negatively interfere with his path. As a result, she kept her thoughts to herself.

6

Prisoner of War

The parachute yanked Pao out of the burning aircraft. A blast of wind pushed him away from his plane as it fell to the ground. It was physically strenuous trying to hold on to the parachute straps. He called out to the ancestors' spirits to protect him. It all happened so fast. After he landed on the ground, Pao felt pain all over his entire body. A few seconds later, he managed to open his eyes and caught a glimpse of the clear sky through an opening in the tall trees surrounding him. The first thought that he had was to run and find a place to hide because this would surely be the location that the enemy would come for him. He rolled over to separate himself from the parachute and tried to see if he could stand up. He had no strength to even crawl so there was no hope of being able to run and hide. What he did manage to do was bring his right hand over to his face. When he touched it, he was relieved that everything seemed to be intact. The sharp pain on his forehead made him feel disoriented. Before he could finish his train of thought, enemy troops surrounded him. The first thing he felt was someone hitting him with a gun. Then, screams came at

CHAPTER 6

him from all directions. He could not understand what they were saying because they were yelling in a foreign language. "They hit me, pushed me down, and tied my hands behind my back. They were very angry! One person pointed a knife at my throat and said many things, but because it was all in Vietnamese, I did not know what was said. Several removed the bullets from their guns and pretended to shoot at me. They continued to kick and hit me. The screaming did not cease until a couple of Vietnamese military leaders who spoke Lao arrived on the scene. They asked me if the soldiers had hit me. I said that they had. The leaders then told me that from then on, they would not let anyone hit me. That was the case. They did not let the soldiers come near me and hit me anymore. But they removed my uniform and cut it into small pieces. Then, they distributed them to the soldiers. I didn't know why they did that. They also removed my shoes." His captors gave him an old black outfit and a pair of cloth shoes to wear. Despite being unable to walk, Pao was immediately tied up. If they knew how he felt physically, maybe they would have saved themselves the trouble, but they did not want to take any chances. Taking a fighter pilot as a POW was a major blow to the enemy, so his captors needed to prevent any possibility that he would escape. Over the course of the war, T-28D bombers had inflicted much damage to enemy forces. Their ability to fly low to accurately hit targets frustrated the enemy. Thus, to have shot down one of them was cause for celebration. Pieces of Pao's uniform served as evidence for these soldiers that they had done so and, perhaps, served as motivation for them to keep fighting.

When he was being dragged away, Pao suspected that he would soon be killed because he heard someone exclaim that they were taking him to be educated. "On our side, when it was said that you were going to be educated, it meant that you would be executed. 'Take him to be educated equals take him to be executed.' We knew the phrase well, so when they said I was going to be educated, I was sure that that death would be coming soon. They said it in Lao [language]. They said, 'Pais hien!' [Go learn!]. 'Chao pai hien!' [You go learn!]. These Vietnamese leaders were politically savvy. They spoke nicely to you. They'd repeated this phrase over and over again, 'We are going to take you to learn and once you are done learning, then you can go home.'" The nice words did not provide any assurance to Pao that he would come out of this situation alive. He thought to himself that even if they did not kill him, he would likely die from the excruciating pain he was feeling. "I didn't know where we were exactly because we kept walking in the jungle."

After a couple of days of walking, Pao realized that they were not going to kill him. They had little to eat, so they gave him a few spoons of rice each day. When they came across a stream, everyone drank from it. Most of the time, his captors appeared to be equally exhausted. "I couldn't walk, so they mainly dragged me." Trekking on foot through thick jungles on steep mountainsides is no small task even when one is physically healthy, but doing so in poor health and without adequate food made the journey even more arduous. After what Pao thought had been thirteen or fourteen days, the group finally reached Nam Kien prison camp in Nonghet, Xiengkhouang province. Nonghet is near the Vietnamese border. It was the village that Hmong settled in when they first migrated to Laos in the mid-1800s.

Pao was extremely tired, but he managed to keep moving because he had no alternative. "As we approached the camp, I heard Hmong screaming and keening from there. Starvation made some of them keen. It was an eerie sound. Once there, all prisoners were forced to wear these cotton uniforms with large numbers on the back. These were outfits for prisoners. I was placed in this prison camp and I would remain until after the cease-fire. I would learn later that there were about one thousand prisoners. It was deep in a valley. They built large,

CHAPTER 6

thatched-roof houses and locked the prisoners up in them. When I arrived, there were about four hundred Thai prisoners of war there as well. The others were Lao, Kmhmu, Hmong, and Yao. They captured these prisoners from a variety of places and brought them there."

One of Pao's fellow prisoners, Nha Yee Thao (Nyaj Yig Thoj), remembered his first sight of Pao in the camp, "I looked at Pao. His face was burned and swollen. I said to him, 'You are here too! You fly in the sky. How did you get here?' He replied, 'My plane was shot down, and they captured me.'" Yee had been in the Plain of Jars, which was a major battleground throughout the war. His company was overrun by enemy troops, which was why he was captured. As someone with a lesser crime, Yee was allowed to go outside. He was observant. After his release, Yee compiled a list of fifty-one Hmong prisoners at Nam Kien. Some died, while others were released and went into exile after the war. Creating the list was Nha Yee's way of not forgetting this dark period in Hmong history.[1]

When Pao first arrived at Nam Kien, the larger war in Vietnam had shifted. President Richard Nixon's Vietnamization strategy of returning fighting in Vietnam to the South Vietnamese army had reduced U.S. troops to slightly more than twenty-four thousand. A few months before Pao's T-28 was shot down, North Vietnam implemented a conventional three-pronged attack against South Vietnam. This March 1972 Easter Offensive sent two hundred thousand soldiers to the south. The United States responded with a full-scale bombing attack against North Vietnam, code-named Operation Linebacker. To prevent North Vietnam from resupplying its troops in the south, American forces used B-52s to drop more than one hundred thousand tons of bombs on North Vietnam during April 1972.

Due to how the war was going at the time Pao arrived at Nam Kien, the prisoners were watched carefully. If people were needed to go fetch firewood, the guards would unlock the doors to the houses and count the number of people they needed. Food was scarce all around. "They used cripples to cook for us. All we ate was expired rice, which was rough. These were rice that the Vietnamese and Chinese had provided to the Lao maybe twenty years ago. They placed some chemical in the rice so that bugs wouldn't eat them. The rice no longer had any flavor. It did not taste like rice at all. You just ate it because it was all that was available. We received a daily ration. Each prisoner was allocated eight kips per day. They would measure the rice bags to determine how many kips and then distribute them to the prisoners. A canned beef that the Vietnamese got from the Soviets . . . would cost 30 kips. So, the 30 kips would be divided among the prisoners, and you received the number of spoons per prisoner depending on how many prisoners were in your group. They boiled the canned beef with water and then served a spoonful to each prisoner, just like when you make offerings to spirits! You would eat this spoonful with your rice. Each table had eight prisoners. They put a large basket in the middle, then pour[ed] the rice into it for everyone. There was one person designated as the leader of each table who would distribute the rice. We had only one broken spoon that had a bamboo handle. The leader would use this spoon to distribute the rice to the eight bowls. He would continue until the rice basket was empty, then that was all [that] each person could eat for the meal." Severe food shortage was the norm in jungle POW camps. It was not only the prisoners who suffered. Pathet Lao guards forced to watch over the prisoners did not have access to much more.

Pao did not expect anything special for himself since all prisoners endured the same harsh conditions. The inability to move around freely was, however, unbearable. "Sadly, we relieved ourselves in the same place that we ate and lived. In the house, everyone had his own can for pooping. You had to find your own bamboo container for pee. A house had 30–40 prisoners.

CHAPTER 6

When you had to poop or pee, you just go when you need to with everyone around you. If you poop a lot and the can is full, then others whose cans had room would share theirs. Around 5:00 P.M. is when we were allowed to go to the river to empty and wash our cans. When someone had diarrhea, we all suffered!" Pao observed that the Lao guards were most vengeful toward the Hmong prisoners. "If the Vietnamese [communists] had been the prison guards, maybe we would have been better off. The problem was that the Vietnamese captured us, but then the prison guards were Lao. The Lao communists treated ethnic Lao, Yao, and Kmhmu better. The Lao prisoners tended to not die in prison because they were allowed to walk around and get a little air. If you do not move around and you are forced to sit and stay in a position all day, you become numb and you can no longer walk. You become swollen. You lose your appetite and you could die. The Lao communists hated we Hmong the most. We were forced to sit in the house all day long. Many prisoners died this way." Despite the poor treatment, Pao made no attempts to escape since he saw the deadly consequences when fellow prisoners who fled were captured.

Although emotionally difficult for him to recount, Pao witnessed five prisoners from his compound pass away. "The illness we had usually began from the feet, then increases to your legs and thigh. Then, you soon can't feel anything. It's like a stroke. When it reaches the stomach, the person would lose the ability to feel. He would not even know that he needed to go to the bathroom. Feces would just come out and fellow prisoners would have to help him wipe them off. One prisoner, Kaying, was sick like that all the way to his neck. His eyes were bulging and eventually became rotten, but he was still alive. He could still talk to you. All you could do was hold his hands. The most difficult part was that you knew that today it was him, and another day it [would] be you. It was a waiting game. There was nothing you could do about it."

Pao remembers another prisoner, Kee Xiong, most vividly. "He and I were sick at the same time. Kee Xiong and I sat next to each other. When his strength deteriorated, he held my hand and he pled, 'Pao, I'm going to die. If you are able to return home, please tell my parents and my wife to sacrifice a cow to release my soul.' Shortly thereafter, he died holding my hand. I cried so hard. My weak body made it seem as though I would be next. There was no medicine. When we asked the guards for medicine, they told us that we needed to be our own doctor. How were we supposed to help ourselves when we were locked up? Where's the medicine? You couldn't even pick leaves!" Anger, frustration, extreme sadness, and hopelessness were daily rituals. There seemed to be no end to the madness. In fact, powerlessness overwhelmed the entire house following Kee's death. "After he died, we wrapped him in his blanket and left him in the yard. There were some rocks and all we did was placed the rocks over him. Not much later, the pigs ate his body. That was the fate of those who died. It was our existence all the way until the cease-fire." Pao was devastated with what happened to Kee's body. To see a fellow human being disposed of in such an inhumane way haunted him for years.

The news that a cease-fire agreement had been reached brought hope to the prisoners. They had been waiting for the day when they each would become food for the pigs, but now a glimpse of hope shimmered. Thoughts of his mother, wife, and son ran relentlessly through Pao's mind. He hoped that they were as he had left them. But so many days had passed by, and frankly he did not know exactly how long he had been imprisoned. He thought to himself that all of this did not matter anymore. He was going to return to his family, and he would put this cruel existence behind him. While the Paris Peace Accord that allowed the United States to disengage from Vietnam was signed on January 27, 1973, the Vientiane Agreement would not be reached until February 21, 1973. The prospect of free-

CHAPTER 6

dom was, however, short-lived for Pao and his fellow prisoners. "There was a time near the end of 1973 when we were going to be brought to the town of Khang Khay to be exchanged for communist prisoners. We were almost there, but they told us that the different factions couldn't agree. They then forced us to walk all the way back to the prison camp. Some of our people died along the way. When asked why, we were told, 'You are Vang Pao's soldiers. They do not have any soldiers to exchange with us. We have you as our prisoners to exchange, but they do not have any of our soldiers to exchange. They did not bring our soldiers that they captured. That's because they executed them all!'" The way of war was such that few enemies were taken as prisoners. If they were captured, they were likely tortured and killed or died while imprisoned.

Realizing how close they were to being set free, Pao and his fellow prisoners could not believe that they were forgotten. Why did this happen? Did the leaders consider them dead? "This was a weak point of our leaders. We, the prisoners of war, suffered so much as a result of following their orders, eating what little roots, flowers, and leaves we could find. The leaders did not even acknowledge our suffering. We were supposed to be home like other prisoners! We couldn't come home then because they killed all of their prisoners." Any hope he had of returning to his family was now shattered. He was sick to his stomach when he thought about the situation. The punishment he endured for a war and its leaders who cared only about themselves was beyond comprehension, as he stated. How could human beings impose such suffering on other human beings?

Following the communist regime's takeover of Laos on December 2, 1975, and the proclamation of the country's new name, Lao People's Democratic Republic, prisoners like Pao were forced to participate in different government initiatives. "I was in a group that went to destroy the buildings at Long Cheng. The homes of the Hmong military leaders at Long Cheng were surrounded by red metal barrels, which were very

72

strong. We tore down all of the homes and buildings, and the materials were brought to Phonsavan to build living quarters for the soldiers there. Long Cheng had no homes standing after we were done! My heart cried out for loved ones that were nowhere in sight, but all emotions had to be suppressed, for if the guards saw, it could have meant death." Not publicly showing emotions became Pao's main survival strategy.

7

Precarious Freedom

In the immediate postwar period, Hmong and other American collaborators who did not flee lived in fear. The new regime often questioned villagers about each other's activities. People became inexplicably cruel to one another. Sometimes men would be taken away simply because other villagers claimed that they were Vang Pao's soldiers. Once accused, no process existed for victims to defend themselves. They were at the mercy of the soldiers who guarded villages. Sometimes guards had to confront villagers who harbored resistance fighters; thus, they too were fearful of ambushes as they patrolled villages. Mutual animosity toward one another created a hostile environment, and as a result, no one could be trusted. Any gesture of kindness from soldiers or fellow villagers were interpreted as means to gather information that could be used against them.

It would be nearly a year later that Pao and his fellow prisoners were freed. "October 25, 1976, was when I was officially released but still lived under tight supervision. There were about twenty of us who were considered to have committed higher

CHAPTER 7

crimes. Six of us were Hmong. The rest were high-ranking Lao officers. We were the last group to be released. We were sent to provide labor for a company called Xenathikan in Phonsavan. We cut down the trees from Phou Keng [mountain]. We then sawed them and sanded the wood so that it would be smooth. We built a thirteen-room building there. It took us close to a year to build it with our own hands. It might still be there today."[1] During the day, Pao also went to work on farms and helped to build bridges.

Pao had no information about the whereabouts of his family, but what was certain was that the hustle and bustle of Long Cheng existed no more. The people he knew and the evidence of one of America's largest covert operations had all but disappeared. Having helped tear down homes in Long Cheng, Pao knew that most people had dispersed. With no options and alternatives, he lowered his head and followed the orders he was given. "The soldiers still followed me everywhere I went. The only difference was that I was no longer locked up." He was relieved to not be cramped up in the thatched roof shelters at Nam Kien. At least now he could go buy food with his meager earnings.

Pao did not earn much from his work. One day, he recalled that when he was captured, he wore a gold bracelet. At the time of his capture, it was taken from him along with his shoes. The Vietnamese military officers at the time told him that they were holding on to his properties, but the items were to be returned to him upon his release. He feared that the guards likely knew nothing about this and that there was little chance that he would get them back. With nothing to lose, Pao decided to go ask the people in charge about his belongings. The guards told him that they would look into it. They also assured him that the items would soon be returned to him. About a week later, he was called in to meet with a military official. The official informed Pao that too much time had passed so they could not locate his belongings. Since they could not produce the items,

PRECARIOUS FREEDOM

he surprisingly offered Pao a sum of money. Pao had expected that he would never get them back, but he certainly did not anticipate any compensation. The twenty thousand kip [about $250] payment was beyond his imagination. On weekends, Pao spent time at the Phonsavan market. After he ate and bought meat and vegetables, he walked around just to watch people going on with their daily life. He often carried out small conversations with the vendors, but they were usually busy trying their best not to let any potential customer pass by their stall without being greeted. Men, women, and children worked from early in the morning until late afternoon when they packed up whatever they did not sell. While some Hmong families lived in Phonsavan town, many traveled from nearby villages to conduct business. Living in town was expensive and limited farmland available required them to travel back and forth. To make the days go by faster, Pao and his friends occasionally asked for permission to visit neighboring Hmong villages on weekends. He used part of the money he received to buy a Western suit. Since few people could afford such items, wearing it implied wealth. Moreover, it suggested that the person who wore such clothing was part of the educated class. This attracted not only young women but also parents who might want their daughters to marry such individuals. Pao and his friends took turns wearing the suit during visits to Hmong villages.

One day, Pao did not want to eat the food in the Morning Market (Talat Sao), so he ventured to a noodle shop a few blocks away. He had previously not done so because he preferred to talk to the Hmong vendors at the market. Most of the businesses in town were owned by ethnic Chinese and ethnic Vietnamese. Expecting the daily routines of small conversations with little meaning, he entered the shop and sat down. The hostess walked toward him and asked for his order. As soon as their eyes met, Pao recalled that tears fell down like raindrops. Remembering that he was still under surveillance, Pao grabbed a napkin and wiped his face as though dust had flown into his

CHAPTER 7

eyes. Standing in front of him was Mrs. Kou Lai (Niam Kub Laij), an aunt from the Yang clan who had married a Chinese merchant living in Laos. When many Hmong fled in 1975, her family left, but she stayed behind with her husband. They were forced to move from Long Cheng to Phonsavan. Business was usually slow, but the small income generated from her noodle shop sustained her family. As though dust had also settled in her eyes, Mrs. Kou Lai wiped her face with her sleeves.

It must have been only about thirty seconds, but Pao said it felt as though it was a lifetime. He managed to pull himself together and ordered the noodle soup (pho). Mrs. Kou Lai headed to the kitchen in the back to prepare his food. He anxiously awaited her return. When she reemerged with the bowl of pho, he took a deep breath before looking into her eyes again. Though only a short time had passed since she left him to prepare the soup, he noticed that her eyes were all red. It was clear to him that she had been crying. She set the pho in front of him and walked away as she normally did with all customers. She did not want to be seen speaking with a stranger. As a married woman with little power, she did not fear much for herself, but she knew Pao's background. She had mourned his disappearance with his wife and parents and had seen how much they had suffered. The last time she saw his wife and parents was in 1975 before they fled. She knew that they had left the country, but she had no way of knowing what had become of them.

Behind the cash register, she pretended to keep herself busy, but all she could think about was the joy of seeing Pao alive, as she revealed to him in future meetings. She did not know if he had received any news of his wife, child, and parents. So many questions went through her mind. She looked up once in a while to see how Pao was doing with his pho. When he put down his spoon and fork, Mrs. Kou Lai approached him and gave him the bill. She placed it in his palm and walked back to the cash register. He looked at it and then placed it in his pocket. He quickly followed Mrs. Kou Lai to the cash register and

PRECARIOUS FREEDOM

paid her. His heart was pounding with joy because he had seen a familiar face, but the frustration of not being able to talk to her was overwhelming. In fact, Pao recalled having very little energy. His head was spinning. At one point, he felt as though he would faint. It took enormous effort to contain himself, for he knew that he could not afford to put her in jeopardy in the event that anyone had been watching him. As normally as he could, he quickly walked back to the small shack that he shared with his roommates.

When the door closed behind him, Pao removed the receipt from his pocket and sat down on the mat. His heart was beating even faster than when he was at the noodle shop. The receipt was very light, but his hand shook as he held it. It had been folded in half so his left hand had to help lift the top so that he could see what was written inside. Even that simple action was nerve-racking for Pao. The note said, "Your wife and child left the country. Your parents left too." His heart swelled with relief. He was overjoyed at the prospect of seeing them again, but at the same time, sadness quickly filled his heart when he thought about the circumstance under which he existed.

He was no longer imprisoned, but he still existed like a prisoner. It had been nearly two years since Mrs. Kou Lai had seen them. How are they doing? Are they even still alive? How big is Pheng now? Is Ong still waiting for him? Does his mother still burn incense every day asking the ancestors to watch over him? With no strength to stand up, Pao lay down on the mat. More questions ran through his mind, and he cried nonstop. He recalled being exhausted, and at different moments, he lost the will to continue living. He does not remember how long he stayed in that position. He was awakened only by the laughter of his roommates who had returned from a visit to the Hmong village. With his back turned toward them, Pao did not acknowledge their presence. Thinking that he was sleeping, they lowered their voices and soon fell asleep. As he lay awake, he replayed flashbacks of the sacrifices his mother made for him,

CHAPTER 7

leaving Ong standing on the roadside thinking that he would be right back to pick her up, and his son, Pheng, who he had held so close to his heart. Surely, Pheng would have no memory of him, and he would not recognize Pheng if he saw him. Thinking about how much time he had lost angered Pao. He wanted to scream to let the world know how much pain he was experiencing, but that would surely draw attention to him. His only choice was to keep his feelings bottled up. It was no use to let anyone know. He cried quietly for a long time before he drifted off to sleep. The next thing he heard was a rooster's crow to let the townspeople know that it was time to begin the monotonous activities all over again.

Pao slowly pulled himself up from the mat. He poured some water from the container into the small kettle he shared with his roommates. After he started the fire in the cooking area, he placed the kettle on the rack. Washing his face with warm water helped get rid of the evidence that he had been crying. He could not share what had happened at the noodle shop with his roommates. They would certainly ask questions that he would not be able to answer without breaking down and crying. Once Pao had washed his face, the first thing that he thought about doing was returning to the noodle shop. He had so many questions for Mrs. Kou Lai. As he thought about it more, he realized that it was probably not the right thing to do. He could go there, but like the day before, he would not be able to speak with her. If he attempted to do so, he may cause her harm for speaking to him. Besides, she may not know more than what she had already told him. He reminded himself that he needed to be cautious. It was especially a dangerous situation because he was unstable. If she did talk to him, he was certain that it would be an emotionally draining conversation. Taking time to reflect before returning to her restaurant seemed to be the best thing to do at that moment. That day, he mostly stayed inside the living quarter.

Although the men still had to obtain permission to go out of town, the surveillance eventually decreased some. The fol-

80

PRECARIOUS FREEDOM

lowing weekend, Pao and his friends decided that they would ask permission to visit Ban Khu, a Hmong village north of Phonsavan town. He was pleased to receive approval for the visit. Pao suspected that the authorities were lenient because he had followed their orders. The friends excitedly traveled by car to Ban Khu, which had a larger population than the contiguous villages. Upon arrival, they paid the driver and then made their way through the village. He was not sure what to expect, but he thought to himself how fulfilling it was to see Hmong men, women, and children joyfully going about their business. As they walked around, he felt someone grab his arm, which startled him. It caught him off guard because he did not anticipate meeting anyone he knew. He turned toward the individual and realized it was Moua Ber (Muas Npawv). As one of the few Hmong teachers, Moua Ber had been a well-known man. Pao was also known to the Hmong in Long Cheng since he had been a fighter pilot. Unconcerned about people seeing a grown man cry, Moua Ber pulled Pao toward him. When Pao's plane was shot down, Moua Ber had mourned his loss with Pao's family. Pao was considered a son-in-law to Moua Ber because Ong was a daughter of one of his Moua relatives. He held on to Pao tightly. Moua Ber could not believe that Pao was standing in front of him. "[Moua Ber] was very emotional. He held on to me and patted my head as though I was a small child. He was family so I also could not hold back my tears. I was so happy to see him!"

In the Hmong village, Pao was not under surveillance as he was in Phonsavan. He followed Moua Ber into his house. There, Pao would begin to recount what had happened to him. He learned about what the Hmong who stayed behind had to endure. Moua Ber did not flee when thousands of others left because he had many children. He could not fight with the crowd to get all of them into the planes during the May 1975 Long Cheng evacuation. Rather than escaping on foot like the majority of villagers, he made a decision to stay. Pao learned

81

CHAPTER 7

that after the communist takeover, Moua Ber's family was relocated to the Phonsavan area. Previously a highly respected teacher, he was now merely a farmer. He shared with Pao that he feared the most for his daughters. The younger was only twelve, so she was safe for now. However, the older two had been forced to go work for the country. Moua Ber explained that soldiers often walked through the village, and when they saw single young women who were sixteen and older, they would require the young women to go serve the country. The exact nature of the work was not discussed openly. Parents who resisted would be accused of being traitors who were not supportive of the new republic.

Pao and his friends had planned to visit only for the day, but having reconnected with Moua Ber, Pao stayed overnight. The two men continued to talk into the night since they had so much to discuss with each other. Moua Ber also confirmed that his wife, son, and parents had left the country, but like Mrs. Kou Lai, he did not know their current status. For Pao, meeting Mrs. Kou Lai and Moua Ber reminded him that since he did not die in prison camp, he must continue to live. After Pao left Ban Khu, he found the courage to go back to the noodle shop. Mrs. Kou Lai served him pho as she had done previously, but this time, they conversed briefly about minor things. "I tried to not look her in the eye when I asked her questions. She would quickly answer me and then go on with business as usual. She'd come back occasionally to ask if I needed anything else, but truthfully, we both knew that she was only trying to talk to me. I told her how I was living, and she seemed pleased to know that I was alive." They did not smile at each other, but inside, each was happy to see the other.

Pao learned that his wife did not remarry and that she had begged military leaders and his fellow pilots to continue to search for him. When Mrs. Kou Lai last saw her and his parents, they were preparing to escape, but indeed she did not know what happened after she left them. Thereafter, Pao would make

82

weekly visits to the noodle shop just to have the small conversations with Mrs. Kou Lai. She was the only relative he had in town. Also, he looked forward to visiting the Hmong village so that he could discuss the war and its aftermath with Moua Ber. Internally, Pao was getting anxious about what to do. He had requested permission from the authorities to be fully released to go live in the Hmong village. He told them that he would like to get married and become a farmer. He made the request twice, and each time, he was denied. Thus, Pao had lost all hope that he would be allowed to live merely as a civilian. He was still existing as a prisoner. It was well-known that many Hmong continue to escape to refugee camps in Thailand. As a result, the authorities were suspicious of people who assembled in groups. Pao suspected that they feared he might try to escape as well. He explained, "The people in charge seemed to have little control of the population. People often slipped away into the jungle and then fought hard to get out of Laos under dangerous conditions." Having spent time in prison camp where he was tortured, Pao had become quite fearful of authority figures. His inclination was usually to not cause any problems. He rarely thought about trying to escape because he feared the potential deadly consequences. Again, that was how he had survived thus far.

Pao's monotonous existence was becoming unbearable, however. He recalled two occasions where he felt extremely sad for women who were still waiting for their husbands. One day, a Hmong woman came to the compound where Pao and the others were kept. She told the guards that she was looking for her husband, Chong Toua Vang (Ntxhoo Tuam Vaj). She had requested to talk to the men to ask if they knew of his whereabouts. Pao remembered, "The guards told us to go outside to see if one of us was her husband. The presence of this woman brought so much joy because she had come to search for her husband. When we went to see her, everyone was sad and disappointed not only for ourselves but for her. She had come

CHAPTER 7

to look for her husband, and he wasn't one of us. We didn't know him." Another woman came not long after also to look for her husband. To the men's chagrin, they had to tell her that her husband had died about two months earlier. He had been sick for nearly six months. "We pointed her to the direction of his grave. She broke down and cried. I was so heartbroken for her and her family! I had helped to carry him to be buried." After she left, the men went back inside. No one said anything because no words could describe how they felt. The women's presence only made things worse. The married men retreated to their living quarters deeply disappointed that the visitors had not been their wives. Each stared at the walls until he fell asleep.

With few activities to occupy his free time, Pao continued to visit the noodle shop. Mrs. Kou Lai greeted him each time he walked through the door. As discreetly as they could, the two continued to exchange words as she served him. The more he visited the noodle shop, the more at ease he became. Perhaps it was only in his mind that people were watching him. He thought to himself that maybe no one had been following him after all. "Thinking back to this period, I'm sure I overreacted. There were only a few guards, so they likely did not have the manpower to follow each of us everywhere. They mostly sat at the office." At the time, however, Pao was certainly not willing to risk it. He revealed that the several years of confinement had made him easily frightened. He was never able to fully overcome the thought that someone may be watching his every move.

When Pao became more comfortable at the noodle shop, he began to talk to other people. Mrs. Kou Lai had employed a sixteen-year-old girl to assist her. Occasionally, Pao tried to have small talks with her. She was usually busy cleaning up after customers or helping out in the kitchen. Their conversations were never longer than the exchange of pleasantries. One day, he noticed that another girl had come to work for Mrs. Kou Lai. This one was younger, and to him, she seemed quite immature. How she went about the noodle shop clearly demonstrated that she had no interest in flirting with men like Pao. She carried on with her tasks. Pao recalled, "This girl seemed irritated with my efforts to talk to her and she made it known to me with her behavior." Each time he attempted to talk to her, she would either quickly answer and then go on her way or ignore him altogether. This continued on for about a week. Pao finally decided that he should stop bothering her since it was clear she had no interest in interacting with him. Moreover, her behavior suggested to him that she did not want to be working at the noodle shop.

The girl's name was Sinxai Moua (Ena's given name), Moua Ber's younger daughter. She had seen Pao at the noodle shop and in the village. Pao revealed that when he visited her parents, he did not pay close attention to who else was in the house. He likely had seen her at their home. However, he never looked at the children closely. This was especially true for the daughters. It would be disrespectful to stare at them in front of their parents. At twenty-nine, Pao seemed like an old man to Ena; she did not pay much attention to his visits to the noodle shop or her parents' home. At the noodle shop, she was concerned about not disappointing Mrs. Kou Lai, for if she did, Mrs. Kou Lai may not be willing to help her parents by employing her. At her parents' home, Ena preferred to play games with the other children instead of conversing with the elders. According to Ena, Pao always seemed more interested in talking to her father anyway.

Once Pao made the connection that the young girl at the noodle shop was Moua Ber's daughter, he told her father that he was interested in courting Ena. Her father had his own reasons for supporting Pao's proposition. As Ena recalled, "Sometimes he would bring me gifts, and I wouldn't even touch them. My parents accepted the gifts, and then other family members would use them. Because he kept showing up at the noodle shop and trying to talk to me, I actually told my parents I did not want to go help out there anymore. My father was upset because he was afraid that if I weren't doing something, the sol-

CHAPTER 7

diers would force him to let me go work for them. Single girls wouldn't have to go if they had a job." To please her father, she did as he instructed. She, however, made no effort to change her behavior toward Pao.

The conversations with Moua Ber, Mrs. Kou Lai, and the two women who came to look for their husbands empowered Pao to change his perspectives about life. In their small living quarter, he and his roommates agreed that they could no longer exist as they had since leaving prison camp. They began to discuss an escape plan from not only Phonsavan but also the country. They had followed all of the rules and had gained the authority's trust that they would not flee. It was then December 1977. The New Year celebrations in surrounding Hmong villages were soon going to take place. It was agreed upon that they would seize this opportunity to leave town for a longer period of time. They had to act fast. Pao recounted the process, "I wrote a letter to the government to ask them to give us permission to go attend the Hmong New Year. We had been imprisoned for nearly five years, and we wanted to visit other Hmong families. After their meeting, they decided to give us permission to go for fifteen days. In Laos [at the time], you had to have written permission like that to travel so that if you are stopped by the police, you will have documentation. I had learned that some of my relatives [who stayed behind] lived near Khang Khay, Khang Khob, and Pha Lai [Pham Laib], such as elder Tong Kai Yang [hlob Tooj Kaim Yaj]." As soon as they received the documentation, the men headed toward the Hmong villages. His younger friends went straight to the jungles. They did not bother attending the New Year celebrations. Pao was afraid that if the officials found out that his friends had fled, they would create problems for him, especially because he was the one who had requested permission for the group. He was sure they would watch him even more closely if he were caught. Or worse, he may even be sent to prison. Pao remembers that he shook excessively as he thought about this possi-

86

PRECARIOUS FREEDOM

bility. Since his friends had fled, he had to take action before someone discovered their plan. With that, he headed straight to Ban Khu village.

Ena remembers playing outside with her siblings and friends when, as usual, Pao showed up. This time he did not come with his friends. Instead, he was accompanied by an elder that she did not recognize. The elder carried an umbrella. Since it was not raining, she knew that this usually meant someone was going to get married. When Pao greeted her, she scurried away from him. Her parents were home, so Pao and the elder entered the house. Ena was clueless about who might be getting married. She thought it was none of her business anyway. What she cared more about was enjoying herself with the village children.

After a short period of time had passed, her mother was sent to fetch her. When told to go inside, she grudgingly followed her mother. Once they were in the house, her father told her that the men had come to ask him for permission for Pao to marry her. She could not believe it when they gave her the news. Ena recounted that she was horrified to learn that. "I was so angry at my father! I did not understand why he would even allow this when my older sister was single. I told him that he should give my sister to them since she was older. I was just a kid, and I didn't even know how to like a boy yet." Unlike many Hmong girls who could not read or write, Ena had attended school. She was literate and outspoken. She often spoke her mind. She pleaded for her father to say no. Since women generally deferred such decisions to their husbands, her mother could offer little help. Ena saw that her mother seemed equally frustrated at not being allowed to support her daughter.

Ena's father told her that it was not up to him or her sister. He told her that even though Pao had a wife, he had chosen Ena. Since polygamy was commonly practiced, this did not seem out of the ordinary for anyone. Her father firmly expressed his desire for her to accept. As she reflected about what transpired, she was certain that the elders had a plan for her.

87

CHAPTER 7

Ena was not allowed to know the details. Even her mother changed her behavior by joining her father and promising her that they would not have to live too far apart after she married Pao. Despite her resistance to the entire ordeal, Ena was a dutiful daughter. She did not want to bring shame to her parents. Thus, she hesitantly listened to them. A small wedding ceremony took place immediately.

Ena was kept in the dark about Pao's plans. As soon as they were married, Ena realized that her mother had made an empty promise. She and Pao had to flee to another village, Pha Lai. Ena could not understand why they had to leave. No one would explain it to her for fear that other villagers may alert the authorities. Many years later, she learned that they fled there to be with one of Pao's uncles, Tong Kai Yang, who helped them escape. On one side of the Nam Seng River were the Hmong Chao Fa resistance fighters and on the other were the Vietnamese and Lao communist troops. The Chao Fa frequently attacked government troops, so they were afraid to cross this river. "But the resistance fighters were our people, so we weren't afraid of them," Pao explained.

Once they left Ban Khu, they had to keep going. There was no turning back. At Pha Lai, Pao searched for his elder uncle Tong Kai. Villagers pointed Pao to his house. As fellow clan members, the two men had an emotional reunion. The rest of his family came to celebrate Pao's return, but everyone was careful not to publicize it too broadly. Villagers were already suspicious of each other. If government authorities knew that they were harboring a fugitive, it could bring trouble to the entire village. If Pao's presence endangered the village, who knew what other inhabitants may do. They could not risk an attack by government forces. Pao had to lay low. Only Tong Kai's most trusted family members knew that Pao and Ena were living with them.

Not long after they arrived, Pao had to make another difficult decision. He recalled, "We were in Pha Lai for a couple of months [when] Captain Vang Bee [former pilot, deceased] and his group returned to assist the resistance fighters. He had heard I was there, and so he asked for me. Informants told him I was at Pha Lai. He sent seven soldiers to deliver a letter to the villagers who [were] fishing. They brought me the letter, which told me to go meet him by the river. I went to meet them, and they were people I knew. They said that since I was alive, they were going to take me with them." Vang Bee had escaped to Thailand, but General Vang Pao told him not to seek permanent refuge abroad. Instead, he was instructed to remain in Ban Vinai refugee camp, where he organized resistance efforts in Laos. He traveled back and forth between Laos and Thailand, and on many trips, he and his men helped to guide villagers to escape. One of the people in the group was Pao's uncle, Youa Chong, and another he knew well was commander Va Chao Yang (Vam Choj Yaj). This brief reunion included news about his family. "They also said that my wife and parents have all escaped to Thailand and that my wife had remarried." This was the first time Pao learned that Ong had remarried. He had hoped that she would still be waiting for him, but he realized that he could not blame her. Besides, he had married Ena before he knew about what Ong had done. He had no time to think about the dilemma. The men pressured him to decide whether he would leave with them.

The group needed an answer on the spot, but Pao could not make up his mind. If he agreed, then he would have to leave that evening. They warned him that this was his only opportunity to escape with them. "At that moment, I was torn and worried. My biggest fear was being caught and killed by the enemy. I had seen fellow prisoners go this route so many times. But I realized that if I didn't go with them, they would never return for me in the future." Pao agreed to leave that evening. The men said they would return after dark to lead him into the jungle. Uncle Youa Chong returned to the house with Pao so that he could help guide Pao into the jungle when it was time to leave.

CHAPTER 7

When he broke the news to Ena, she was extremely unhappy. She felt betrayed in so many ways. She stated, "I listened to my parents and went with him because they had promised me that they would stay near us. They said that I should help Pao work hard and prepare for when they joined us at Pham Lai. Now, we were going to go away and they did not know anything about it!" She had no news from her parents since they left Ban Khu. If they were going to leave, Ena wanted to at least let them know. Ena did not know that her parents were aware of Pao's plan to escape. They had allowed Pao to marry Ena so that he would take her out of the country. Since she was kept in the dark, Ena was afraid that if things became difficult along the way, Pao might desert her. How could she trust him? She was confused. He told her that it was a life and death situation. They needed to leave that evening, or they may not have a chance to do so again. The anger she felt turned into fear. Why could they not wait until her parents arrived at Pham Lai? Pao knew that he and her parents had deceived Ena, but he could not afford to wait another day. He told her to gather the few belongings they had. That afternoon they stayed inside to avoid having to interact with other villagers. They also bid farewell to Tong Kai's family knowing that they will not be able to talk when they leave.

As soon as darkness fell, Uncle Youa Chong told them to get ready to go. He helped them with their belongings. They exited the house and quickly disappeared into the jungle. Once they were on the move, Pao remembered being unsure of the decision he had made. "I knew it was necessary for us to leave if we wanted any chance of living a better life, but I was afraid that something horrible would happen to us. If we ran into government soldiers, we would surely die!" Ena added, "The truth is that I did not fully understand what was going on. There I was! Barely thirteen and I was going into the darkness with a man my parents forced me to marry and another man who I had just met earlier that day. What was I supposed to do?

It was so dark in the jungle that you couldn't see anything in front of you." She held on to Pao's shirt so that they would not be separated. They followed closely behind Uncle Youa Chong. After a short time, Uncle Youa Chong informed Pao that they had left the government side to enter the Chao Fa controlled area. Their destination was a village called Thang Khai (Thaab Khaib) near the highest mountain in Laos, Phu Bia. Located relatively close to Long Cheng, Phu Bia's thick jungle enabled Hmong resistance fighters to hide. It was there that tasseng (county chief) Sai Shoua Yang (Xaiv Suav Yaj) and his soldiers continued to engage with government forces.

The several months that they spent at Thang Khai was difficult. In contrast to villages in government-controlled areas where people could grow their own food, those living among Chao Fa fighters had little to eat. Government troops tried to get them to leave the jungle. This required the fighters and their families to frequently move from one area to another. They survived mostly by foraging and hunting wild animals. Pao was not sure how much longer they could survive living like that. He left Pham Lai with the hope of getting to a place where he no longer had to worry about perpetually looking over his shoulders. The living condition at Thang Khai was worse. He consulted with Vang Bee about the situation. Vang Bee had escaped to Thailand with his family. They remained in the refugee camp while Vang Bee followed General Vang Pao's orders to organize resistance forces inside Laos. He encouraged Pao to seek refuge in Thailand where thousands of refugees waited for opportunities to permanently settle in foreign countries. Vang Bee made it clear to Pao that he was going to stay and continue the fight. Frustrated by the inability to quell resistance fighters, Lao government forces were increasing efforts to force them out of the jungles. This included the sporadic bombing of Hmong villages.

When Pao made up his mind to leave, others decided to join him, including Uncle Youa Chong. They searched for rice to

CHAPTER 7

buy from nearby villagers. Once they had gathered enough for the journey, they prepared to say goodbye to those who would stay behind. This was especially heart wrenching for families who were forced to separate. Ena recounted the predicament that Uncle Youa Chong and his wife confronted, "It was the saddest thing to observe! His wife was pregnant and would be due soon, but he didn't want to leave her behind. She walked for a little while, but she couldn't keep up. They both cried and decided that she would stay behind. They'd walk away from each other, but then he'd run after her. They did this several times until she made up her mind that she would go back to the village because she did not want to have the baby in the jungle." Although the child was born not long after the group departed and his wife eventually escaped to join him in the refugee camp, that day Youa Chong left with a heavy heart. Ena described his facial expression as somber for most of the journey.

After their small group parted from the Chao Fa at Thang Khai, they joined another group that was escaping at the same time. Pao recalled this about the escape, "There were fifty-one people in our group. We walked for fifteen days from Phu Bia Mountain to the Lao/Thai border. I had to carry enough food for the both us. I carried thirty-three cans worth of rice, a gun, and a water container. We passed through areas with unexploded ordnance. Crossing rivers and going through Yao and Kmhmu villages. My wife was young and very small. Through thick paths and across bridges, sometimes I carried her in my arms and other times on my back. Because she was very young, she couldn't carry anything heavy. Her main task was to carry her few pieces of clothing and an inflatable tube for us to use when crossing the Mekong River."[2] The treacherous journey was the reason why the elderly and families with small children often stayed behind. It took a toll on even healthy individuals. Limited access to food and water caused some travelers to be ill. They had packed what they thought would be enough to last them until they reached the Lao/Thai border. Even though they had the guidance of people who had previously escaped to Thailand, Pao said that they almost ran out of food. "On the evening that we tried to cross, we were down to our last pot of rice. That evening was scary because if we couldn't cross, we'd have no more food."

As they got closer to the border, the escapees became increasingly anxious. Tired and hungry, some doubted their ability to safely reach Thailand. Many had heard tragic stories of bandits preying on powerless escapees and soldiers shooting indiscriminately into groups. They hoped that they would avoid such encounters. Pao continued, "As we passed the village that stood between us and the river and stepped on the rice paddies, dogs barked loudly. Since it was four in the morning, the sound of cow and horse bells increased our fear even more. You could see traffic on the Thai side increasing." Since few Hmong could swim, many had drowned while attempting to cross this river that divided Laos from Thailand. If they crossed during the rainy season, the situation could be deadly. It was October 31, 1978, when his group reached the river. Although the monsoon season had passed, the water was still relatively high.

Prior to the escape, Uncle Youa Chong had connected with some local Vietnamese and bought an inflatable tube from them. Ena initially carried the tube, but when Pao's load lessened as they consumed the rice, he added it to his. When they reached the Mekong River, they confronted a major obstacle. Pao explained how they resolved the issue, "Since we did not have anything to pump air into the tube, my uncle and I took turns blowing air into it. Once there was enough air, we placed a small piece of wood in the valve to prevent the air from being released. We had each carried a long bamboo log just for the purpose of using it to cross. We placed the two bamboo logs together, then we tied the tube on top of them." Because the tube was the size of a large tire, Ena said she still cannot believe how Pao and Uncle Youa Chong managed to blow enough air into

CHAPTER 7

it. She exclaimed, "I suppose when you are desperate enough, you can do incredible things!" This task seemed to have been small in comparison to the crossing. Among the escapees, the soldiers were mostly single men. They easily lay on top of their bamboo logs and swam across. Pao stated, "As for me, I had four people: my wife, my father's younger brother [Youa Chong], and my cousin. I had to drag all three of them!" Several families were in similar situations. Once they had prepared the equipment that would enable them to attempt the crossing, each slipped into the water and followed Pao's instruction to the designated position. "My wife lay on top of the tube, my cousin hung on one side and my uncle on the other. I was in the front and I pulled them. Before that moment, I had never thought about how big the Mekong River was. Everyone said go into the water, so we just did it. You could tell the current was very fast, but you tell yourself that you do not have any choices, so dead or alive you must go. Even though the river appeared to be as vast as the sky, I kept going." Like those before and after him, Pao was determined to reach safety at any cost.

For Pao's group, the crossing was not smooth sailing. Instead, the fast currents forced the raft to flip over twice. When the two bamboo poles split apart the second time, Pao had to quickly pull them and place them between his legs. "I continued to swim and dragged my family. The problem with the tube was that at the beginning, it kept pulling us backward because of the currents. Once we passed the fastest currents in the middle of the river, then it floated forward, toward the other side. We didn't go straight though. We floated down the river for about a mile before we reached the other side." Of the group that arrived at the border and crossed together, Pao remembers that two people died. One was a grandmother and the other was a newborn who drowned during the crossing. The heartbroken parents had to leave the child's body in the river in order to save themselves. To make matters even worse,

94

PRECARIOUS FREEDOM

the mother's sarong drifted away at that time. She was naked when she reached the riverbank. She remained there until local monks brought her a new sarong.

When everyone had reached the Thai side, the first thing they saw was a group of Thai soldiers waiting for them. Pao recalled, "We weren't sure what they would do to us. We were told to sit down. A short time passed before the local people generously brought food to the group. Thai border patrols really didn't care about us, but we were fortunate because they did not abuse us." After he had settled in the United States, Pao heard other escapees recount horror stories of bribery, physical violence, and rape by Thai border patrols. He pointed out how fortunate his group had been that no one encountered such tragedies. After they ate, the group sat and waited. Then, several trucks arrived, and they were instructed to climb into them. "We were taken to a site called Meung Kaan. That night, we slept on the ground just like a bunch of pigs. Not a single blanket! We stayed there for several days before they could prepare documentations for us to enter Nong Khai refugee center." Although Pao's group encountered some setbacks, their crossing was not out of the ordinary. In fact, their journey was representative of the experiences of thousands of refugees who fled Laos after 1975. What was extraordinary about this particular crossing was that Pao had escaped death.

8

Return from the Dead

For over a year after Pao's aircraft was shot down, Ong and her mother-in-law held numerous shaman ceremonies asking the ancestors' spirits to protect him. They used pieces of clothing that he had worn to represent him during the ceremonies. When he did not return after other POWs were released following the February 21, 1973 cease-fire agreement, all hope of Pao ever returning disappeared. His family had to spiritually let him go. Close relative Yang Chee recounted, "As customary in Hmong animist traditions, a soul releasing [tso plig] ceremony had been carried out by our Yang clan for Pao." This Hmong cultural practice is the final step in the life cycle. The living perform the ritual to officially let go of the deceased's soul and encourage it to continue on its journey to the other world. When Pao reemerged at Nong Khai refugee camp six years later, it was as if he had returned from the dead.

Once the group had all descended from the trucks, an announcement was made over the loudspeaker that a new group of refugees had arrived, an activity that occurred frequently

CHAPTER 8

from the late 1970s throughout the 1980s. The announcer encouraged camp residents to go to the center to see if any were their relatives. Pao recalled that as he and the other new arrivals entered the camp, many people greeted them. It was chaotic. As the crowd approached the group, Ena's aunt, Nou, recognized her. She forced her way through the crowd to grab her niece. The women hugged, cried, and talked about all of the suffering they had endured and how much they had missed each other. Why was Ena alone? What happened to her parents? After a brief update, Aunt Nou led them to her living quarter and began preparing food for them.

Pao and Ena had just sat down to eat when the camp director made another announcement. Through the loudspeaker, he excitedly broke the news that pilot Pao Yang was alive and that he was now in the camp. Most people who lived in Long Cheng knew about Pao's unsolved disappearance. Immediately after the broadcast, people rushed to the camp office hoping to see him. "My relatives flocked to the camp center, but because there were so many people, they did not know where I was. Another voice came through the loudspeaker, 'Pao Yang, where are you now? We want you to know that we are looking for you. Please let us know where you are!' When we heard that, Aunt Nou led us back to the center." The loudspeaker was the main communication vehicle in the refugee camp. In addition to news of all sorts, it was how refugees learned when their resettlement applications had been approved. Thus, people paid close attention to all announcements.

Once Pao and Ena reached the center, some of Pao's relatives who had been living in Nong Khai ran to him, including another uncle, Za Thao Yang (Zam Thoj Yaj). "More members of my extended family came, and it was now our turn to cry!" The relatives and other camp inhabitants surrounded him and hugged him. The crowd grew and one after another patted Pao and told him how much they missed him, including strangers he had never met. Uncle Za Thao grabbed Pao and held onto him tightly as though he was afraid Pao might disappear if he let go. Both men were so emotional that it took a while before Uncle Za Thao could compose himself. When he managed to get some words out, he told Pao that they had been waiting for news of his whereabouts for years.

Ena watched as young and old camp inhabitants expressed joy of seeing Pao alive. She had not known the details of Pao's past. Her parents may have mentioned it to her, but she was too distressed to pay much attention. She had seen Pao as merely a man who had convinced her parents to force her to marry him. Because of his actions during the escape, she believed that he loved her, but she was still bitter about him making her leave the country without telling her parents. Since she thought that he was just an ordinary man who had tricked her, Ena was perplexed about why a mob had encircled her husband. She recalled that moment as filled with confusion. "At that time, I just thought that it was a normal thing that happened when people arrived in the refugee camp. I just stood still with my aunt while people surrounded him. There were so many people that I lost sight of him for a while. People just pushed their way into the crowd to get a glimpse of him. I think they wanted to see it with their own eyes, that it was really him!" It was in the refugee camp that Ena began to learn more about the person she had married. Seeing how much people respected him changed her opinions of Pao as well. No longer was she bitter; instead, she was proud to have married someone people considered a hero.

After a tearful reunion, the four new arrivals stayed with Uncle Za Thao. A few days later, Pao was called in to meet with Thai officials. "I do not know how the Thai officials knew, but someone must have informed them that I was there. During the meeting, they asked me some questions about being shot down and my experiences as a prisoner of war." He briefly answered

CHAPTER 8

the questions that they posed and chose not to offer the details of his suffering. It would take too much time and more importantly, he was not ready to talk about it. They let him go. Pao soon learned from his relatives that his parents were living in another refugee camp, Ban Vinai. They also told him that his wife had remarried and resettled in the United States with her new husband, but that his son, Pheng, had stayed behind with Pao's mother. All he could think about was letting his mother and son know that he was alive and that he had returned safely. "I wrote a letter for a brother-in-law, Moua Houa, to take to her." Although his mother, Sua, was not literate, the relative promised to read the letter to her.

Pao shared what his mother told him upon receiving the news that Pao had arrived in Thailand. "She told me that very early the next day, she held my son's hand and went to bribe the Thai guards, which was the only way for refugees to get permission to leave the camp. With enough money, they will usually prepare the documents to ensure that you safely pass any checkpoints along the way. The next morning, they put her and my son in the front seat of a car. They were then on their way to search for me at Nong Khai."

It took Sua and Pheng about four hours to reach Nong Khai camp. "When they arrived at our living quarter, I was not there. It was only my wife." Since his mother did not know his new wife, Sua immediately returned to the center and pleaded for the people in charge to make an announcement. Over the loudspeaker, the announcer exclaimed, "Pilot Yang Pao. Your mother has arrived! Wherever you are, come to meet your mother. She is here!" Pao had anxiously waited for this great news. When he heard that she had arrived, his heart started to beat faster as he ran to the center. The announcement played over and over in his mind. "This was the hardest moment for me. I cannot describe how great I felt about seeing my mother again. She thought that I had died. It's almost like being born all over again, and I'm now going to meet my mother. She

100

RETURN FROM THE DEAD

Grandmother Sua and Pheng were very close since she raised him. (Photo courtesy Ong Moua)

was a great mother! I was her life. When I was shot down, Pheng was only eight months old. He was then seven. I knew that seeing them again would be the best, yet most difficult, thing."

As Pao made his way toward the center, other inhabitants of Nong Khai refugee camp followed suit. They also wanted to witness the mother and son's reunion. When he arrived, a large crowd had gathered. "When I saw her and Pheng, I was overjoyed, and yet my heart ached so much. My mother held me in her arms as though I was still a small child! She was crying so hard, but she managed to tell me that not a day had gone by that she didn't think about me. She wondered how I was and [told me] that she asked the ancestors to watch over me and that if I were alive, she asked the ancestors' spirits to help lead me back to her. I also held on to my son Pheng. He had no memories of me except for what he had been told by his mother and grandmother." Pao remembered the crowd hovering over them. There was barely enough room to stand because they all wanted to hear what Pao had to say. It seemed like they expected a great performance.

The reunion was probably a disappointment to those who wished to hear what he had gone through during the previous

101

CHAPTER 8

six years. He could barely speak. With his mother caressing his head and expressing how grateful she was to the ancestors, Pao wept continuously. His mother exclaimed, "Kuv tus me tub es! Niam nco koj ua luaj! Ua tsaug lub ntuj! Ua tsaug poj koob yawm txwv coj kuv tus me tub rov los cuag kuv!" (My dear son! I have missed you so much! Thank you to the heavens! Thank you to the ancestors for bringing back my dear son to me!) He could not speak one complete sentence. Everyone at the scene cried along with the mother and son. Many likely had lost loved ones, so they wept not only for Pao but also for sons, husbands, fathers, and nephews who could not return from the battlefield.

After what seemed like hours of the mother and son holding each other in front of hundreds of spectators, both were finally able to wipe off their tears and speak to each other. They had six years to catch up on, but now that they were back together, the most important thing was to figure out what to do next to ensure that they would never be separated again. Pao did not waste any time. "I went to ask the guards for permission to leave the camp. The documentation was required because we were not Thai citizens and did not have any paperwork to travel in the country. The next day, they approved for me to go with my mother to Ban Vinai camp."

Since his father was living with his third wife that he married in the camp, he did not receive the news at the same time. It also took him longer to get permission to go to Nong Khai. He arrived after Pao had already left with his mother. Upon discovering this, he returned to Ban Vinai. In addition, one of Pao's uncles, Xia Sher Yang (Txhiaj Sawm Yaj), also obtained permission to travel from Ban Vinai to Nong Khai. Unfortunately, the bus crashed on the way there. He was not seriously injured, but he was forced to return to Ban Vinai.

About a half dozen camps had been established to receive refugees fleeing Laos. Ban Vinai refugee camp continues to

102

play a significant role in Hmong historical memory. From the fall of 1975, when it was first established, through when it closed in the early 1990s, it was the largest concentration of Hmong refugees. Located fifteen miles south of the Mekong River in a valley surrounded by rolling hills, its size was slightly more than a square mile. In May 1975, the CIA had evacuated a couple of thousand individuals from Long Cheng to another military camp, Namphong, a base where some Hmong pilots had practiced flying during training. As more people fled on foot after the evacuation, the military barracks were not adequate to house the increasing number of refugees arriving each day. Thai authorities decided to relocate the refugees to this valley. Ban Vinai was managed by the United Nations Border Relief Operation (UNBRO) and supported by nongovernmental organizations (NGOs). While some equipment and supplies were provided, the refugees had to help construct the buildings. Cutting down vegetation and building homes as they had always done in Laos transformed Ban Vinai into a village of more than forty thousand inhabitants by the mid-1980s.[1]

When Pao reached Ban Vinai, camp authorities once again announced that pilot Pao Yang had arrived. The fact that people were not sure whether they should believe the announcement sparked their interest even more. Everyone in the camp who heard the announcement rushed to see if the downed pilot had indeed returned. Those who were related to him and those who knew him personally pushed through the crowd to get to him, a scene similar to what had occurred in Nong Khai. Pao remembers being overwhelmed with people wanting to talk to him once the crowd saw that he was alive. After some time, the satisfied crowd dispersed, allowing Pao and his family to go to the section of the camp where his mother had been living. A smaller group followed them inside her dwelling.

CHAPTER 8

The days and weeks that followed Pao's arrival at Ban Vinai were both chaotic and heart wrenching. He received visitors continually. They wanted to hear what had happened to him. He recalled, "Pilot [Lue Lee's] older brother came. For days, he would come over to talk to me, starting around six in the morning. Family members of my fellow pilots who were killed in action came too. Friends and relatives touched, hugged, and caressed me. They cried excessively with sadness and joy. Their teardrops fell on my clothes. The only thing that did not happen was that they did not keen."

Pao understood their pain and did not mind their visits. "All of this in the name of love. Widows whose husbands were captured, imprisoned like me, . . . and never returned came. Parents whose sons disappeared came. Those whose sons died in the war and [had already been buried] came as well. They often talked about how fortunate I was to return and how their sons were not able to return. For example, pilot Ly Tou Xiong and I knew each other very well. When I was shot down, his family was sad for my mother because I was gone. Ly Tou Xiong was killed after me, and in the end, I returned to my mother. They were very sad about the situation because he was not able to come back like me. But all of this is fate. Life is really just about fate. One group after another would come because in the camp, there was not anything to keep us occupied. Day and night, it didn't matter too much." Pao recounted bits and pieces of his time in prison camp, but he avoided some of the most horrific moments because he had not yet come to terms with what he had endured.

The visitors also asked if he saw or heard of their husbands or sons. "In some cases, I could help them. That's because in the prison camp, I was the only pilot, but there were [also many] Hmong soldiers. Some of the Hmong soldiers were people I knew. When I was taken to the prison camp, I saw them, and they saw me. We would approach one another, and tears always filled our eyes. But the guards did not allow us to talk to each other. They watched us closely and if they saw us talking to each other, they would pay closer attention. It could be deadly, so we all mostly just stared at each other." Silence helped him and fellow prisoners stay alive, but now everyone with whom he interacted requested that he speak.

Family and friends were not the only ones who demanded Pao's time. "Colonel Vang Neng had asked me to go meet with him. The Thai officials also met with me. The American officials who visited refugee camps often called me to go meet with them. So, I basically met with different people day after day. I was asked to talk about what happened when I was shot down." Visits of this nature continued for about two months, during which time Ena existed as though she did not have a husband. Although Pao was extremely busy, he was not immune to the hardship of camp life. Like the other refugees, his family experienced food shortage and challenges with the living conditions. He decided to find a way to leave Ban Vinai. "Jerry Daniels [the last CIA advisor to Vang Pao] and Charlie were the people in charge. I do not remember Charlie's last name. I told Charlie and Jerry that I didn't want to stay in the camp anymore. The hardship was unbearable. I asked if I could leave soon. But they wouldn't let me. They asked me to stay and help them process resettlement applications because there were so many Hmong refugees."

Pao could not say no to them because thousands of desperate refugees were waiting to go somewhere. Anywhere. Thus, he agreed to stay for one year. He was placed in charge of the third section with a caseload of close to three thousand people. In addition to serving them, Pao often participated in meetings with international visitors, in particular United Nations High Commissioner for Refugees (UNHCR) representatives interested in assessing camp conditions. When American folk singer Joan Baez visited refugee camps in Thailand in October 1979, Pao met with her and the other delegates to discuss his imprisonment and camp conditions. International visitors helped

Joan Baez visited the refugee camp when Pao was a staff member helping to process resettlement applications. She gave him this autographed photo of herself, 1979. (Pao Yang and Ena Yang collection)

Pao speaking to international visitors at Ban Vinai Refugee Camp, 1979. (Pao Yang and Ena Yang collection)

RETURN FROM THE DEAD

raise awareness about camp conditions and encouraged support for resettlement programs, but on the frontline, Pao witnessed many persistent problems.

Despite his desire to alleviate some of the camp inhabitants' suffering, Pao believed that it was impossible to do the job well. "No food and limited mobility—there were so many problems we encountered. Sometimes I'd still be in bed and they would already gather near my house waiting for me to sign paperwork for them to go work as day laborers for nearby farmers. It's very hard to leave the camp to find work without the permission slip. Sometimes people would sneak out of the camp to cut down trees or look for firewood, and Thai authorities arrested them. Women were raped. Young men and women were beaten and robbed. Those with cows didn't watch them carefully, so they would go eat the neighbor's vegetables. New arrivals would come and sit around me to wait for when they could get food. I ran around just trying to resolve these kinds of issues. Lack of resources made taking care of them very difficult. You couldn't succeed because you had no more than the people you were trying to help." He became overwhelmed by the perpetual powerlessness and decided that the confinement inside the camp was no way to live.

9

A Second Chance

As the year came to an end, Pao had helped process all of the people in his section for resettlement to another country. He accomplished what he had agreed to do, so he decided to ask Jerry for permission to leave the camp with his family. This time Jerry agreed, but there was another obstacle. His father had three wives. Those with multiple wives were not allowed to go to the United States together. General Vang Pao was allowed to enter the country with his several wives because of strings that the CIA pulled, but ordinary Hmong refugees did not have the same privilege. Despite his problematic relationship with his father, Pao did not want to leave him behind. He consulted with Jerry, who devised a solution. "Jerry advised me to have my mother divorce my father and then she could apply for resettlement with me. That was the only way that my whole family could resettle. Thus, I prepared the document and Jerry signed that my parents were divorced. She and Pheng came with me. My father and the minor wife were a separate household. The middle wife resettled as a widow with her children. That was how my entire family was able to come to America in December 1979."

CHAPTER 9

Pao helped to deceive immigration officials about his family composition. It is not something that he is proud of, but it was for survival. He believes that the end justified the means. Food had become increasingly scarce and housing was overcrowded. The number of refugees waiting in Thai camps had increased greatly following the 1978 Vietnamese invasion of Cambodia, which impacted the conditions for other refugees from Laos. Since refugees could not resettle in the United States until American sponsors willing to host them had been secured, it prolonged the stay in camps for many. A broader issue was that the number of sponsors could not keep up with the demands as "compassion fatigue" among Americans increased due to what seemed to be a never-ending dilemma. Extended families typically were separated as a result of sponsor availability.

Ena did not want to leave the refugee camp because she had hoped that if they waited, her parents and siblings may one day escape to join them. She recalled being conflicted when Pao informed her they would have to go to the United States. "By then our daughter Ta had been born. I still missed my parents and siblings so much, but now that I had a child. I had to think about her life." Even though she had become a mother, Ena said that because of her young age, everything was confusing. "You are told that you're going to America, but you had no way of knowing what America was like." Similarly, Pao had no knowledge of the place where he was going to and how he would support his family. But he was hopeful. Anything seemed better than just existing in the camp.

Because of their dire existence, Pao feared that staying longer would drive him crazy, as he described. He could barely feed his family with the rations provided by camp officials. He knew that returning to Laos was not an option then, or in the near future, and living a life without any direction in the camp was no better. He decided that he would not just sit and wait for a sponsor to be found by immigration officials. To speed up the process, he wrote to ask for help from a brother-in-law,

A SECOND CHANCE

Family photo in Ban Vinai refugee camp. Left to right: Grandmother Sua, Pao, Pheng, and Ena (carrying her and Pao's oldest daughter, Ta), 1979. (Pao Yang and Ena Yang collection)

Chai Yang Moua (Caiv Yaj Muas). Chai Yang Moua was Ena's cousin who had settled near Pittsburgh, Pennsylvania, a few years earlier. Upon receiving the news, Chai Yang worked with five local churches to serve as sponsor for Pao's large family. Pao was thrilled when Chai Yang wrote back that a solution had been found.

During the days leading up to when they loaded the bus that always took refugees from the camps to the Bangkok International Airport, Pao and Ena prepared themselves for the

CHAPTER 9

journey. Ena remembered, "I didn't have much to pack so everything fit in a suitcase. They were just clothes." Like other refugees, they possessed very little.

Refugee departures were always emotional for the ones leaving and those left behind. Pao and Ena had watched the same scene play out over and over again for nearly a year. For once, they knew what the moment would be like when it was their turn to leave. When the day arrived, the bus pulled up to the loading area. Pao and Ena picked up their belongings and made their way to get in line with other families who had also been approved to leave the camp. Once the suitcase had been placed on top of the bus, they turned back to the tearful relatives who would be left behind. After they had said their goodbyes, Pao gestured for Pheng to go in the bus. Pheng, his mother, sister, and nephew climbed up the steps to find seats. Ena held their daughter and followed them. Pao came after a few minutes and sat down next to Ena. Having been in Bangkok a few times during pilot training, Pao was aware of the hustling and bustling of its people who seemed to be rushing to get to somewhere. He thought about his people being so unfamiliar with this life and a harsh reality set in. He and his fellow refugees were on their way to the unknown. The thought made him deeply sad and he fought to keep tears from falling. There were confused faces in front of and behind him. No one was smiling. In fact, some cried loudly, while others silently wiped away tears. The somber atmosphere was unbearable, and his heart ached in a way that he had felt so many times during the years of imprisonment. Pao closed his eyes for a brief moment. His entire being was overtaken with emptiness. Only Ta's sweet cry letting Ena know she was uncomfortable in the heat filled the immense void and brought him back to the present.

At the airport in Bangkok, the refugees were herded to the waiting area to be further processed. One by one, they went through the lines. Few people talked to each other since it was difficult to say anything without breaking down. Silence was

112

A SECOND CHANCE

each person's friend. Children clung on to parents for fear of getting lost in the crowd, not realizing that their parents were equally disoriented. When all had been seated in the aircraft, Pao turned to look at Ena, Pheng, Ta, and his mother. A great sense of relief came over him. During most of the two-day, arduous journey, Pao drifted into and out of sleep, and occasionally memories of his own flying experiences flashed by. Most of the time, he just stared at the clouds through the window. Although confined in the aircraft, he felt free.

The family landed in Chicago, Illinois, on December 28, 1979, along with a small group of fellow refugees. Exhausted and disoriented, they deplaned with other travelers. Pao held tightly onto the plastic bag that the International Office of Migration provided. It contained the necessary paperwork to get them through customs. Once inside the terminal, the new arrivals were directed to gates from which they would be sent to wherever their sponsors lived. Saying farewell to the other refugees seemed even harder. Ena stated, "On the way from Bangkok, it was tiring and scary, but at least you still saw other Hmong people on the plane with you. The flight from Chicago to Pittsburgh was terrifying because every direction you turned, there were mostly white people. Some of them looked at you strangely!" This was their first time being a racial minority. She thought the bizarre stares were likely because they had not seen many people like them. Ena assumed that fellow travelers may have considered them strange, but she thought they were odd-looking people too. Since Hmong considered looking people in the eyes as rude, she remembers looking down each time she saw someone staring at them. They were very tired from the long international flight, so soon after takeoff on the domestic flight, the family members fell asleep.

When they landed in Pittsburgh, the American sponsors and Chai Yang were waiting for them. Seeing a familiar face in a strange land brought great joy to the new arrivals. Pao's and Ena's tears of sadness were transformed to joy when they re-

CHAPTER 9

The family arrived in Pennsylvania in 1979. Back left to right: *Sua, Pao (carrying Ta), and Ena.* Front left to right: *Thai Yang (cousin), Pheng, and See (cousin). In their new home, Pao and Ena finally smiled. (Pao Yang and Ena Yang collection)*

united with Chai Yang. He, too, was glad to see them, for it had been a lonely existence, as he later shared with them. The sponsors combined resources to help Pao and Ena start their new life. Pao praised them because they came from small congregations with modest means. He asserted, "In this country, it is the churches that cared about people like us. We Hmong have to be grateful to the churches. We must not forget their generosity and God's grace." Some sponsors hosted refugees temporarily in their homes, while most typically secured housing of varied quality for them. In Pao and Ena's case, the sponsors had rented a house. Following the gracious reception at the airport, they were escorted to their new home.

Their American life began in the small town of Freeport, Pennsylvania. The sponsors had brought some food. After they showed them how things worked in the house, the sponsors

A SECOND CHANCE

left the family to rest. Everyone was extremely tired. Because of jet lag, they were wide awake at night and could barely open their eyes during the day. This went on for about a week, during which different church members took turns to check in on them. The visits by church members and Chai Yang's family helped them adjust, but Pao and Ena confronted a situation that motivated them to search for a difference place to live. Pao recounted, "After two months in the country, I had chicken pox. It was so bad that the sponsors would not allow me to sleep in the same room with my wife and kids. There were bumps all over my body, so they were afraid that it would be contagious. Even I was afraid just looking at myself! I stayed home for about two months. There was even a local newspaper article about my chicken pox!" To make matters worse, the sponsors did not allow Chai Yang's family to visit them. This made Pao and Ena feel abandoned. To Pao, Chai Yang was all he had to lean on. "My family was so lonely and to some extent, hurt. We had no car. There was just us, but he didn't visit me when I was sick. The Americans were afraid that my illness was contagious. We Hmong we do not care about that. He didn't come. His children were not allowed to visit my children. My wife and I were saddened by all of this. In the Hmong way, we would not do that. Even though they told my wife and I not to sleep together, we still did it, and she did not get sick." This seeming lack of care from his brother-in-law was one of the reasons why Pao ultimately began searching for another city to move to, though first he had to provide for his family.

Pao felt helpless because there were seven people in his family. He became desperately worried about how to support them. As soon as he recovered, the sponsors found him a job, which he accepted without hesitation. "My first job was working for the city. I picked up trash and trimmed trees along the streets." It was not the kind of work he had envisioned for himself, but he put forth his best effort because the family's survival depended on his actions. He had no one to complain to since even

CHAPTER 9

his sponsors seemed to not have much themselves. It seemed, however, that this was just the beginning of a series of obstacles that his family would face in their new country.

If it were just the unsatisfying job and loneliness that his family experienced, they may not have tried to move. Pao recounts, "We lived in a nice home, but it was haunted. The stairs from the second floor faced our bedroom door. At night after everyone has gone to bed, someone would walk down from the second floor all the way to the front of our bedroom door. At first I thought it was a burglar, so I crawled to the door and listened carefully. When I was near the door, there would no longer be any movements. As soon as I returned to my bed, then I heard someone going up the stairs. My family was so scared. We weren't Christians yet, so we did not know about God. The next day we told our sponsors that there was a ghost in the house. The sponsors were more afraid! The next night, we turned on the lights and went upstairs. Nobody was there, and we became even more scared." Pao was emotionally distressed with the situation. Ena noted that she was afraid because of what Pao told her he had seen, but she herself did not hear or see anything.

After three months, Pao no longer wanted to stay in Freeport. The haunted house, the disappointment at his brother-in-law's neglect during his illness, and the tremendous pressure to find more suitable employment to meaningfully support his family overwhelmed him. On one occasion, he had gone with Chai Yang to visit the Hmong families who had settled in Pittsburgh. While there, he heard that Yang Chia (Yaj Txiab) and Cha Pao Moua (Tsav Pov Muas), who were also relatives, lived in Reading, a small town northwest of Philadelphia. As soon as they could, he and Chai Yang traveled to Reading to visit them. Pao stated, "Yang Chia was a FAC [forward air controller]. He was a mechanic who fixed our planes, so he knew me well. They said that because there were few relatives, I should move to live closer to them. I told them that I would move if they came to help me. They agreed to come to help me move

116

Pao and Ena tried their best to adjust as quickly as possible into U.S. society. (Pao Yang and Ena Yang collection)

so my family and I packed as fast as we could and left Freeport." Having a few more Hmong families helped to reduce the isolation, a process that many refugee families followed that eventually led to the establishment of large ethnic enclaves in several states.

In Reading, Pao recalled that they continued to struggle financially, especially before he found a job. "The support we received from the government was very minimal. It was not enough to feed all of us, so I went to work. I found a job that paid $3.10 per hour. Even with some food stamps, we still could not survive on this job, so my wife found a job too. She found a sewing job which paid $4.00 per hour. After tax, our $7.00 combined salary was just enough to pay bills. Fortunately, our rent at the time was only $280.00 per month." Pao and Ena tried their best to make ends meet, but after a little over three

CHAPTER 9

years, they decided to move to another state. This decision set in motion their way of life for the next several decades. The first move in 1983 was to the Midwest. "My father and his other wives had settled in Michigan. Shortly thereafter, they moved to Appleton, Wisconsin, to live near Uncle Xia Sher [Yang] (Txhiaj Sawm). I decided to follow them to Appleton. Once there, I tried enrolling in a job-training program at the technical school, but it was too difficult, so I was not accepted. We then moved to Sheboygan [Wisconsin]. The program I enrolled in was not only hard, but also the teachers were exceptionally harsh on us." A growing number of Hmong refugees were relocating to Minnesota and Wisconsin to join family and friends who were employed in manufacturing jobs. In the early 1980s, families whose refugee cash assistance was terminated were sent by social service providers to apply for public assistance. Young, able-bodied men and women who had some education took advantage of the opportunity to enroll in education and training programs while receiving welfare benefits. Pao discussed how such opportunities helped them gain work skills: "We knew we didn't want to be on public assistance, but we also knew that if we didn't get more education, we would not be able to find good jobs. The public assistance was a temporary support to help us get our lives together." While Pao enrolled in technical programs, Ena took English as a second language (ESL) classes. Since she was young and literate in Lao, learning English was not as difficult, but Ena did find it challenging. Teachers wanted their students to gain English language skills that would enable them to find jobs within eighteen months; thus, they had pressure to ensure that students learned.

Their interpretation of the teachers' strict rules was not all negative. Pao and Ena viewed it as part of their Americanization process. In fact, they applied to become American citizens as soon as they became eligible. As legal immigrants, the law allowed them to go through the naturalization process after five years. They were motivated to learn and rebuild their lives and they saw citizenship as a means to enjoy the benefits of becoming American. Although Pao was not interested in giving himself a Western name, he asked one of his teachers to help choose an American name for his wife. Pao explained, "The teacher chose the name Ena for my wife. So Ena Yang became her legal name for a while." Interestingly, influenced by her passion for Thai culture, Ena eventually changed her name again. Pao added, "It is a Thai name, Charunee. Her last name is different too! It's Mongthavekul." Charunee Mongthavekul would subsequently replace Ena Yang as her legal name. She continues to use Ena with family and friends, however. The changing of her name seems to symbolize Ena's grappling with her identity as a young girl whose childhood was lost when she became a wife and mother at age fourteen.

The search for something better and more meaningful at all costs became an integral part of Ena's and Pao's life in the United States. Throughout the 1980s, 1990s, and 2000s, moving from state to state across the country would become their way of life. By the second decade of the twenty-first century, they had lived on the East and the West Coasts, as well as in the Midwest and the South. When the small town of Sheboygan did not fulfill the family's dreams, Pao looked for a larger city that would provide more opportunities. "While my family lived in Sheboygan, I commuted to Milwaukee to attend Milwaukee Area Technical College. I graduated with a degree in machine shop in 1987."

He did not find a job after graduation, but shortly thereafter, he heard about a program in Georgia that helped refugees with job placement. Relatives from the Moua clan had visited Georgia to find out if it were true. When they returned, they recommended that Pao move to Georgia with them. The refugee program had resources to not only help with moving expenses but also provide rent for a couple of months after they settled in the state. Two weeks after they arrived in Georgia, both Pao and Ena found work. Even though their income was

Pao was determined to support his family by pursuing higher education so that he could have a new profession. He graduated from technical college with half brother Chai Va Yang (Nchaiv Vaj Yaj). (Pao Yang and Ena Yang collection)

MILWAUKEE AREA TECHNICAL COLLEGE

PAO YANG

HAS COMPLETED IN A SATISFACTORY MANNER THE PRESCRIBED CURRICULUM FOR

Machine Shop

AND IN TESTIMONY THEREOF IS AWARDED THIS

Diploma of Graduation

Dated at Milwaukee, in the State of Wisconsin, this Third day of June, Nineteen Hundred and Eighty-Six

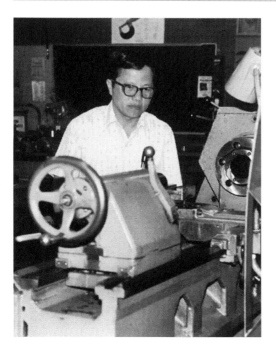

Pao earned an associate degree from Milwaukee Area Technical College in 1986. (Pao Yang and Ena Yang collection)

Pao worked on and off in machine shops until he became ill and had to retire. (Pao Yang and Ena Yang collection)

CHAPTER 9

still relatively low, they finally felt as though they were making noticeable progress. Four months later, they bought a house. Pao said, "During this time, we worked very hard because we wanted to have a good life. My wife worked full time during the day and then contracted with different sewing companies for projects during the evening. This was necessary just to sustain our family because our jobs each paid only $5.00 an hour." Pao and Ena exemplify the hard work ethic common among many new immigrants and refugees.

Their jobs provided adequate income for survival, but they desired more. They had dreams of owning their own business. In 1992, an opportunity opened up for them to acquire a travel agency in Chamblee, Georgia, which is northeast of Atlanta. They bought Thai Travel and added a gift shop. At one point, they reached four thousand customers. "We employed two Thai agents to assist with the travel agency and hired several more to work in our shop. We sold and rented Thai movies." While Ena focused on the business, Pao worked full time so that they would have health insurance for the family, which by then included two more daughters and one son. Everything seemed to be going in the right direction.

As they pursued their American dream, however, Pao and Ena found themselves with little time to spend with their five children. Grandmother Sua took care of the house and the children while they worked. She had always supported Pao, and so caring for her grandchildren was her joy in life. They gave her a sense of purpose, and her contribution allowed Pao and Ena to thrive in their jobs. Their success enabled Pao and Ena to better financially support their family. Although they had limited time to enjoy with their children, they were pleased with their ability to provide opportunities for them. The three girls participated in a Thai classical dance troupe, and Ena thoroughly enjoyed the comments that instructors and other parents made about her daughters. Ena recounted, "Every time they performed, people would congratulate me about how good

122

Pao's children in 1988. Front: *Madala;* middle row, left to right: *Kalia, Ta, Vaug;* back: *Pheng. (Pao Yang and Ena Yang collection)*

my daughters were. They were graceful and beautiful. Some parents even told me that they couldn't believe the girls were Hmong! They had thought my daughters were Thai." Such comments stemmed from the historical stereotypes of Hmong as a primitive ethnic group. Ena did not let it get to her. She interpreted their remarks as mere jealousy.

CHAPTER 9

Ena and Pao loved to travel whenever they had a chance. In 1993, they vacationed in Cancun, Mexico. (Pao Yang and Ena Yang collection)

The gratification of parenthood would soon be shattered as the girls fell victim to the challenges that confronted Hmong and other Vietnam War refugees in the late 1980s and early 1990s. Truancy, delinquency, and gang-related activities spread across the different communities in the United States as their American-born children struggled with their bicultural lives. Ena ran the business all day, and Pao helped out after work. They became too busy. When the children asked them to go places together and to attend their activities, they could not fit them into their hectic schedules. As a solution, they allowed the girls to go with friends. Not long after, they became involved with the wrong crowd and made some unhealthy decisions. In addition to a strained relationship with Pheng, who had reconnected with his birth mother, her children's behavior causes Ena to recall those years with much disappointment. "I am not trying to shame my family. They are lessons I've learned, and so I'm just trying to talk about what went wrong. Pheng became bitter and did not want to give his siblings rides. The girls began to stray away from what we had taught them. It was chaos! Gangs from California and Minnesota came to Georgia. Cambodian gang members recruited my youngest daughter, Madala. She brought them to our house, and a few days later, our house was burglarized. We suspected them and told the girls they could not have their friends over to the house. The older two, Ta and Kalia, got angry and ran away. They did return after a few days because they could not survive."

The problems did not go away. When Ta turned seventeen, Ena and Pao sent her to live with Ena's mother in Minnesota. Ena's parents had by then escaped and immigrated to the United States. Her hope was that it would help Ta to stay away from the gang members in Georgia. She added, "In Minnesota, Ta met Vang Xiong, a Hmong boy who she eventually married. The sad part was that we were thinking that she would get away from the thugs in Georgia, but we did not know she would meet another gangster there. Vang was involved with the gangs in Minnesota, but he had supportive parents. Because of some gang problems, Vang's life was in danger, so we brought Ta and Vang back to Georgia. I think this saved their lives!"

Their second daughter followed a similar path. Kalia became involved with Cambodian gang members. Ena recounted, "I was so frustrated that I brought my daughter to Thailand with the intention of leaving her with my Thai friends. When we got there, she refused to stay so we came back home togeth-

CHAPTER 9

er. As soon as we got back, she snuck away to be with her gang members and became pregnant. She was only fourteen! When we moved her to Minnesota with her Cambodian boyfriend in the late 1990s, more problems overwhelmed us. Kalia went to school and when he saw her talking to a Hmong boy, his Cambodian thugs beat him up, and that started a war with the Hmong gang. He was arrested and went to jail. When he got out of jail, he took Kalia, and they went back to Atlanta. Kalia didn't stay with him long and returned to Minnesota with the baby, who was born premature so had a lot of health issues. We helped her out as much as we could. As luck would have it, she met a Lao man and soon had a child with him. He did nothing meaningful, stayed up all night and slept all day!" Ena's revelation about her daughters' involvement with gang members is not unheard of. Although it was more common for boys to join gangs, many Hmong families also faced similar challenges when their daughters were lured into such activities.

Ena's and Pao's heartaches did not stop there. Their youngest daughter, Madala, had been a good student. They had much hope for her since she finished high school and enrolled at Saint Catherine's University in St. Paul, Minnesota. That hope, however, began to fade not long after she started college. One day, she told them that she wanted to move out of the dormitory into her own apartment, but she did not allow them to help her. They later discovered that her African American boyfriend was living with her and that he neither worked nor was in school. Madala dropped out of college, and the two of them moved to Florida. Although Ena and Pao spoke on the telephone with Madala from time to time, they had not seen each other in years. When Pao, Ena, and Ena's mother visited Florida and contacted Madala, she would not meet with them.

After five years in the business, they sold Thai Travel in 1997 and moved back to Appleton, Wisconsin, to once again search for new business opportunities. They did not sell the house and instead, transferred it to Pheng. He was expected

126

to work and pay the mortgage. They took the three daughters and left Pheng and Vaug with Grandmother Sua in Georgia. Vaug shared that his parents had wanted him to move with them. Even though only fifteen at the time, Vaug felt that it was wrong for his parents to leave Pheng, so he chose to stay with his half-brother and grandmother. Vaug remembers the incident and reveals its lasting impact on his life. "They just left. I was just a kid. I had to learn to take care of myself. They were gone for fifteen years! Pheng was a father figure to me. He was the provider even though he struggled himself." The brothers remain close.

Once back in Appleton, Pao and Ena opened another travel agency called Bangkok Travel. They offered passport preparation services and sometimes led tours to Thailand. Since few Hmong had international travel experiences, they helped them with predeparture information for trips to Laos and Thailand. Ena stated, "We taught them how to complete the various forms, such as arrival and departure documents. We also talked to them about differences across airlines. For example, if they flew Korean Air, they would have to board a bus to get to their departure gate when they changed planes in Korea. This information helped them to not get lost."

These predeparture educational services were minor. Sometimes they had to deal with very complex travel issues. Pao recalled one of the most challenging circumstances they faced: "One particular situation was when a man from Appleton died while visiting Thailand. His parents, wife, and kids were in Appleton. This man from the Thao clan went by himself. He died from food poisoning. They wanted to bring his body back to Appleton to be buried. A cadaver traveling internationally is more complex than a living person! Even though the body was placed underneath, it still needed all of the proper documentations such as passport. We had to help make arrangements, but U.S. customs needed reason of death. We called to have the papers prepared, but when the letter came, it was in Thai, which the

CHAPTER 9

immigration officials did not understand. We had to pay for the translation of the explanations in Thailand; then, it had to be faxed to Los Angeles before the body could be flown to Minnesota. Family and friends were all waiting at the funeral home for the body, but when it arrived at the airport in Green Bay, officials there would not let the body through because of problems with documentation. They sent the body back to St. Paul so that it could be returned to California. The entire process would have to begin all over again. Fortunately, we were able to get more information from abroad to be submitted to officials in Minnesota. It took several hours for the body to be flown back to Green Bay. When it arrived, the funeral home staff and family members were able to go pick up the body." Similar to many immigrant businesses, Ena and Pao catered primarily to their ethnic community. As community members opened similar travel agencies, competition became fierce.

Despite their continued hard work, business did not go well. They closed the agency and moved to St. Paul in 1999. Hmong entrepreneurs were very active in the Twin Cities; however, Pao and Ena had had enough, so they decided not to get involved. Pao found a machine operator position that enabled them to make ends meet. In 2003, his health deteriorated. He had to undergo heart bypass surgery. "In fact, I didn't know I had problems, so I actually went straight from work to the surgery room. Following the surgery, I did not return to work. I've been retired since then, but my wife continued to look for better opportunities." Before he fell ill, Pao did not regularly visit the doctor's office. He was not interested in telling anyone how he felt. If he had no physical pain, then he did not see a need to do so.

When Pao regained his strength, he and Ena packed up and headed to the West Coast. Ena exclaimed, "We had wanted to travel and see other places, so in 2006 we moved to Santa Ana, California." She became a real estate loan officer, but soon thereafter, when the industry began to fall apart, they moved

128

A SECOND CHANCE

to Sacramento. "In Sacramento, we didn't have jobs, so we opened a deli business. She cooked and I delivered the food to different Hmong grocery stores. After a while it became physically difficult for me because I couldn't carry heavy loads. After four months, I suggested to my wife that we close this business too." Ena is a skillful chef and enjoys cooking a variety of Asian dishes. She would have preferred to invest more time in this business, but she complied due to Pao's health.

Ena's next move was to become a life insurance agent. Her determination helped her get established. As Sacramento has the third-largest Hmong concentration in the United States, she thought she could thrive there. Like the travel agency, the intense competition prevented her from making a living. In 2010, they packed up and left Sacramento for Siloam Springs, a town of fifteen thousand people in Northwest Arkansas. They had relatives engaged in the poultry industry. Hmong Americans from different parts of the country relocated to Arkansas, Oklahoma, and Missouri to buy poultry businesses on many acres of land. The lower cost of living appealed to Pao and Ena. Most of the families who moved to southern states were small farmers, so few offered other types of services. Although the Hmong population was smaller, there was also less competition. Ena decided to give life insurance agent another chance, but she confronted setbacks since families either already had life insurance policies or they could not afford them. Once again, this business endeavor did not go as she had envisioned.

Ena's last major effort was resorting back to her sewing skills. In Arkansas, she opened an alteration shop. Customers drove miles to have her sew Lao- or Thai-style outfits, especially for special events. Because of the small clientele and the fact that farmers worked hard with little time to socialize, this business did not generate enough revenue to support them. She closed the shop after three years. Although they had occasionally returned to visit, it was then fifteen years since they left Georgia. They had run out of business ideas. To their chagrin,

CHAPTER 9

no other location appealed to them. But the truth of the matter was that they were getting older. Pao's health condition had not improved. Their return to Georgia in 2013 was not without drama. No longer able to hold stable jobs, they resorted to living with Vaug and his wife in Winder, Georgia. As a dutiful son, he welcomed them back into his life, but he made it clear that he had no interest in their parenting advice. He softly stated, "They've been back and forth during the last five years, but it's difficult at times to have them back in my life. That's because sometimes I feel like they treat me as though I'm still fifteen. I have my own priorities, and I prefer to just take care of my family, go fishing and things like that. I don't want to do all these community activities that they want me to do." Vaug has come to terms with his traumatic upbringing. A father of young children, he and his wife do welcome Pao's and Ena's help. Knowing that the lost time can never be recovered, the parents and child are learning to coexist and, to the best of their abilities, make meaning of what is left of the life they have together.

As for Pao's first wife, Ong, she had moved on with her life. She said that Pao had written her a letter shortly after he arrived in the refugee camp, but it was full of harsh words accusing her of not being faithful to him and abandoning their son. Ong rationalized that his action was based on the fact that he did not know the truth. "He has no idea how much I suffered. I thought he died when I remarried. I wanted to take Pheng with me, but his mother begged me not to. She said, 'I already lost my only son. If you take Pheng, then please wait until I die before you remarry. If you leave me now, then please do not take my grandson. If you take him, then I do not want to live.'"

Upon learning that Pao had returned, Ong struggled emotionally and psychologically. To know that Pao was alive but that he had a new wife was hurtful. She had remarried because she thought he had died. When she received the news, she had already started a family with her second husband in California.

130

One of the few times that the parents gathered with their children and grandchildren. Left to right: Son Vaug, Pao, Ena (behind grandsons), daughter-in-law (Pheng's wife), Pheng, and Ong. (Pao Yang and Ena Yang collection)

Since both had new spouses who preferred that they not meet, Pao and Ong could not reunite. Ong and her second husband eventually divorced. She expressed much sorrow that a chance encounter with Pao in Minnesota during the mid-1990s resulted in hard feelings between her and Ena. As the drama unfolded, Ong decided to lessen her communication with her son, Pheng. When the children from her second marriage relocated to Georgia, Ong was pleased. She moved there with them. Finally, she and Pheng lived near each other and were able to rebuild their relationship. Vaug and Pheng had tried to gather the family a couple of times, but the awkward interactions discouraged them from continuing to do so. Both are focused on doing the best for their own families. As for the parents, unresolved tensions remain, resulting in intentional efforts to avoid each other at community events.

10

"I Lived to Tell My Story"

> The activity of remembrance, and the creation of the topoi
> of collective experience which it entails, are irrepressible.
> They express some fundamental truths about the tendency
> of ordinary people, of many faiths and of none, to face the
> emptiness, the nothingness of loss in war, together.
>
> —Jay Winter

A core condition among human beings across time and place is that of suffering. Human beings' inhumanity to other fellow human beings cut across race, class, ethnicity, gender, and geographical locations. In exploring Pao's humble life, suffering has been magnified only because of the dreams and aspirations of great nations to amass political and economic power at all costs. In their quest to dominate others, powerful nations often forged ahead without plans in place to deal with the aftermath. The twentieth century saw a greater number of atrocities than any other period in world history, and we are living its enduring legacy at the beginning of the twenty-first century. Pao is among the nearly two million people who sought refuge in the Western Hemisphere following the Vietnam War—or American War, as the people in Asia call it. His escape narrative and the trial and error of starting life all over in a foreign land are certainly not unique. On the contrary, they reflect the central narrative among forced migrants dispersed across the globe: loved ones left behind, memories that refuse to go away despite

CHAPTER 10

the passage of time, extreme and sometimes harmful behaviors that are attributed to long-standing pain and sorrow that have never been given the chance to heal, and the agony that comes from yearning for the things that will never be.

What does Pao make of his life experiences? Hindsight is twenty-twenty. Would he make the same choices had he known how his life would turn out? Maybe. Maybe not. Life is complex. Is America an adequate prize? Pao has mixed feelings: "America is a prosperous country but parallel to this prosperity is a condition that is equally stressful. When I was preparing to depart for the U.S., it was like going into the darkness with no sense of direction. I felt like I had no choice but to go forward. It was similar to the time that we crossed the river. The Mekong River glimmered with strong current, but you needed to go so you descended into the water. In your mind, you say that if you died, then you die, but if you don't, then you will get to the other side and face the unknown head on." It seems that having survived the sharp vicissitudes of life should make Pao bitter and that he would speak forcefully about the iniquities. Instead, the soft tone of his voice during our many hours of conversation, in addition to his tendency to speak in the third person, suggests that he is trying to distance himself from his harrowing past.

Were the sacrifices worthwhile? The only way for Pao to keep moving forward is to believe that he, his fellow pilots, and others who gave their lives did so for a greater purpose. He considers himself a bit old-fashioned. He believes in fate and that the unintended consequences are equally as important as what one hoped to achieve in the first place. He reflected, "If war had not come to us, then there never would have been any opportunities for our people to set foot in this country. Our children would not have the educational opportunities that they do now. I risked my life so that my people could have a bridge out of misery. In Hmong, we say, 'Sacrificing your life is

"I LIVED TO TELL MY STORY"

Pao was honored at the 2002 Veterans Day in Oklahoma. Congressional Medal of Honor recipient Herschel Woodrow Williams shakes hands with Pao to thank him for his service. (Pao Yang and Ena Yang collection)

better than allowing your people to perish' [Yus txojsia tu zoo dua li yus haiv neeg tu]. Our sacrifices made it possible for us to come to this country. So, for the living, it was worth it." But for the dead, Pao is at a loss for words.

Does he think about the enemy that died from bombs he dropped? "I did think about them then and now. There were times when I wondered why we were bombing them so much.

135

CHAPTER 10

Pao reunites with fellow former pilots in Sheboygan, Wisconsin, in 2014. The Aviation History Center of Wisconsin restored a T-28 aircraft that had been used to train Lao and Hmong men. Left to right: *Captain (Retired) Pao Yang, Captain (Retired) Koua Xiong, Lieutenant (Retired) Phong Yang, Major (Retired) Vang Kha, Lieutenant (Retired) Tou Vang, Captain (Retired) John Bounchanh Sayavong, Lieutenant (Retired) Ya Lee, and Captain (Retired) Foua Vang. (Photo by Victor Vaj)*

I did wonder about that, but then you saw them killing your pilot friends and other people. There was so much destruction, so you tell yourself that it's OK. You have to do whatever it takes. You did not know how many people died from the bombs you dropped." He thinks war is complicated and that no one wins. That is because only those who survive have the privilege to reflect on its impact on them. Whether they were friend or enemy, the dead cannot speak. Only the living get to speak for the dead. He had held the hand of a dying man until he took his last breath and buried fellow prisoners. Having been so close to death many times does not make it easier for Pao to speak about the subject.

Was it fair that he suffered so much for so long? Pao has had his share of misfortunes. He views the misery he endured as a result of bad luck. "My luck in this life has not been very good because I experienced more than my share of hardships, but the one good thing is that God let me live. My enemies had buried me under the ground, but I did not die. My superiors neglected me then and after I returned from prison camp. They made no attempt to acknowledge my sacrifices, but through it all, I survived. A higher being greater than any of them was watching over me. I lived to tell my story."

When he thinks about what he has endured so far, Pao appreciates simply having been able to live his life. "I'm at the end of my life. I wish happiness to those of you who read my life story" (*Kuv lub neej twb yuav kawg. Kuv xav kom nej cov uas tau nyeem txog kuv lub neej tau txais kev zoo siab*). This process of remembering old wounds, reflecting and accepting the things that he could not control during the course of living, forgiving himself for the harmful actions that he took, and working toward dismantling the prison walls that had plagued his very existence has helped Pao to find some peace. In the end, he wishes only the same for all who turn these pages.

Notes

INTRODUCTION

1. In April 2019, Oxford University Press published my book, *Fly Until You Die: An Oral History of Hmong Pilots in the Vietnam War*. It was based on the more than forty oral history interviews I conducted regarding the Water Pump Program.

2. See Nicholas Tapp, *Sovereignty and Rebellion: The White Hmong of Northern Thailand* (New York: Oxford University Press, 1989); Jean Michaud, "From Southwest China into Upper Indochina: An Overview of Hmong (Miao) Migrations." *Asia Pacific Viewpoint* 38, no. 2 (August 1997): 119–30; Christian Culas and Jean Michaud, "A Contribution to the Study of Hmong (Miao) Migrations and History" in *Hmong/Miao in Asia*, ed. Nicholas Tapp, Jean Michaud, Christian Culas, and Gary Yia Lee (Chiang Mai, Thailand: Silkworm Books, 2004), 61–96.

3. See Erika Lee, *The Making of Asian America: A History* (New York: Simon and Schuster, 2016); Shelly Chan, *Diaspora's Homeland: Modern China in the Age of Global Migration* (Durham: Duke University Press, 2018).

4. Robert Jenks, *Insurgency and Social Disorder in Guizhou: The "Miao" Rebellion, 1854–1873* (Honolulu: University of Hawaii Press, 1994).

5. James C. Scott, *The Art of Not Being Governed: An Anarchist History of Upland Southeast Asia* (New Haven: Yale University Press, 2009), 18.

6. See Arthur J. Dommen, *The Indochinese Experience of the French and the Americans: Nationalism and Communism in Cambodia, Laos, and Vietnam* (Bloomington: Indiana University Press, 2002), and Mai Na M. Lee,

NOTES TO THE INTRODUCTION

Dreams of the Hmong Kingdom: The Quest for Legitimation in French Indochina, 1850–1960 (Madison: University of Wisconsin Press, 2015).

7. See Seth Jacobs, *The Universe Unraveling: American Foreign Policy in Cold War Laos* (Ithaca: Cornell University Press, 2012).

8. See Jacobs, *Universe Unraveling*, for a comprehensive history of U.S. foreign policy toward Laos.

9. Paul Hillmer, *A People's History of the Hmong* (St. Paul: Minnesota Historical Society Press, 2009), 82.

10. Major John C. Pratt, *The Royal Laotian Air Force 1954–1970*, HQ PACAF Directorate, Tactical Evaluation Contemporary Historical Examination of Current Operations (CHECO Division), 7th AF, DOAC (September 15, 1970), 4.

11. For a detailed history of Hmong pilots' experiences in the Water Pump Program, see *Fly Until You Die*.

12. See Madeline Y. Hsu, *The Good Immigrant: How the Yellow Peril Became the Model* (Princeton, NJ: Princeton University Press, 2017), and Ellen Wu, *The Color of Success: Asian Americans and the Origin of the Model Minority* (Princeton, NJ: Princeton University Press, 2013).

13. Mimi Thi Nguyen, *The Gift of Freedom: War, Debt, and Other Refugee Passages* (Durham: Duke University Press, 2012).

14. Katherine Bowie, "Palimpsests of the Past: Oral History and the Art of Pointillism," *Journal of Asian Studies* 77, no. 4 (November 2018): 855.

15. Louis Starr, "Oral History," in *Oral History: An Interdisciplinary Anthology*, ed. David Dunaway and Willa Baum (Nashville, TN: American Association for State and Local History, 1984), 11.

16. Bowie, "Palimpsests of the Past," 858, 861.

17. Ibid., 856.

18. Paul Thompson, "History and the Community," in Dunaway and Baum, *Oral History*, 41.

19. Jacquelyn Dowd Hall, "Documenting Diversity: The Southern Experience," in Dunaway and Baum, *Oral History*, 190.

20. Alistair Thompson, "Making the Most of Memories: The Empirical and Subjective Value of Oral Histories," *Transactions of the Royal Historical Society* 9 (January 1999): 291.

21. William Schneider, *So They Understand: Cultural Issues in Oral History* (Logan: Utah State University Press, 2002), 106.

22. Lynn Abrams, *Oral History Theory*, 2nd ed. (New York: Routledge, 2016), 54.

23. Ibid., 153.

24. Mark Cave, "Introduction: What Remains-Reflection on Crisis Oral History," in *Listening on the Edge: Oral History in the Aftermath of Crisis*, ed. Mark Cave and Stephen Sloan (New York: Oxford University Press, 2014), 5.

25. Ibid., 5.

140

NOTES TO CHAPTER 7

26. Ibid., 11.
27. Ibid., 8.
28. Schneider, *So They Understand*, 77.
29. Thomson, "Making the Most of Memories," 292.
30. Thompson, "History and the Community," 40.
31. Abrams, *Oral History Theory*, 79.
32. Ibid., 33.
33. Cave, *Listening on the Edge*, 3.
34. Schneider, *So They Understand*, 79.
35. Abrams, *Oral History Theory*, 106.

CHAPTER 1

1. When Bounchanh Sayavong became a U.S. citizen, he changed his first name to John. He was the only ethnic Kmhmu pilot.
2. Hmong and Kmhmu pilots who served between 1968 and 1972 completed a high number of combat missions largely due to the fact that enemy forces were nearby. Some days a pilot could complete four or five missions because from takeoff to when they released the bombs and returned to base could take about an hour.
3. Thadeua Road had many shops and restaurants.

CHAPTER 2

1. John M. Duffy, *Writing from These Roots: Literacy in a Hmong-American Community* (Honolulu: University of Hawaii Press, 2011).
2. This has become the primary writing system that is used throughout the diaspora and in Southeast Asia today.
3. Manynooch Faming, "Schooling in the Lao People's Democratic Republic," in *Going to School in East Asia*, ed. Gerard Postiglione and Jason Tan (Westport, CT: Greenwood Press, 2007), 171–98.
4. Ibid., 177.
5. In 1962, US $1.00 equaled 80.00 Lao kip. Thus, 5,000.00 kip would have been about $62.50.
6. Faming, "Schooling," 175.

CHAPTER 6

1. Yee Thao gave this author a copy of the list of Hmong prisoners of war at Nam Kien.

CHAPTER 7

1. Phou Keng Mountain is northwest of Phonsavanh town. It is part of the vast Plain of Jars.

141

NOTES TO CHAPTER 7

2. The distance from Phu Bia Mountain to Nong Khai, Thailand, is about 165 miles. It took more than two weeks because of the harsh walking conditions and escapees typically could not walk during daylight. Yao and Kmhmu are two of the nearly fifty ethnic minority groups in Laos.

CHAPTER 8

1. Lynellyn Long, *Ban Vinai: The Refugee Camp* (New York: Columbia University Press, 1993).

Bibliography

Abrams, Lynn. *Oral History Theory.* 2nd ed. New York: Routledge, 2016.

Bowie, Katherine A. "Palimpsests of the Past: Oral History and the Art of Pointillism." *Journal of Asian Studies* 77, no. 4 (November 2018): 855–77.

Cave, Mark, and Stephen Sloan, ed. *Listening on the Edge: Oral History in the Aftermath of Crisis.* New York: Oxford University Press, 2014.

Chan, Shelly. *Diaspora's Homeland: Modern China in the Age of Global Migration.* Durham: Duke University Press, 2018.

Culas, Christian, and Jean Michaud. "A Contribution to the Study of Hmong (Miao) Migrations and History." In *Hmong/Miao in Asia*, edited by Nicholas Tapp, Jean Michaud, Christian Culas, and Gary Yia Lee, 61–96. Chiang Mai, Thailand: Silkworm Books, 2004.

Dommen, Arthur J. *The Indochinese Experience of the French and the Americans: Nationalism and Communism in Cambodia, Laos, and Vietnam.* Bloomington: Indiana University Press, 2002.

Duffy, John M. *Writing from these Roots: Literacy in a Hmong-American Community.* Honolulu: University of Hawaii Press, 2011.

Dunaway, David K., and Willa K. Baum, eds. *Oral History: An Interdisciplinary Anthology.* Nashville, TN: American Association for State and Local History, 1984.

Faming, Manynooch. "Schooling in the Lao People's Democratic Republic." In *Going to School in East Asia*, edited by Gerard Postiglione and Jason Tan, 170–206. Westport, CT: Greenwood Press, 2007.

Hall, Jacquelyn Dowd. "Documenting Diversity: The Southern Experience." In *Oral History: An Interdisciplinary Anthology*, edited by David Dunaway and Willa Baum, 177–188. Nashville, TN: American Association for State and Local History, 1984.

BIBLIOGRAPHY

Hillmer, Paul. *A People's History of the Hmong.* St. Paul: Minnesota Historical Society Press, 2009.

Hsu, Madeline Y. *The Good Immigrant: How the Yellow Peril Became the Model.* Princeton, NJ: Princeton University Press, 2017.

Jacobs, Seth. *The Universe Unraveling: American Foreign Policy in Cold War Laos.* Ithaca, NY: Cornell University Press, 2012.

Jenks, Robert. *Insurgency and Social Disorder in Guizhou: The "Miao" Rebellion, 1854–1873.* Honolulu: University of Hawaii Press, 1994.

Lee, Erika. *The Making of Asian America: A History.* New York: Simon & Schuster, 2016.

Lee, Mai Na M. *Dreams of the Hmong Kingdom: The Quest for Legitimation in French Indochina, 1850–1960.* Madison: University of Wisconsin Press, 2015.

Long, Lynellyn. *Ban Vinai: The Refugee Camp.* New York: Columbia University Press, 1993.

Michaud, Jean. "From Southwest China into Upper Indochina: An Overview of Hmong (Miao) Migrations." *Asia Pacific Viewpoint* 38, no. 2 (August 1997): 119–30.

Nguyen, Mimi Thi. *The Gift of Freedom: War, Debt, and Other Refugee Passages.* Durham, NC: Duke University Press, 2012.

Pratt, John C. *The Royal Laotian Air Force 1954–1970.* HQ PACAF Directorate. Tactical Evaluation Contemporary Historical Examination of Current Operations, CHECO Division. 7th AF, DOAC, September 15, 1970.

Schneider, William. *So They Understand: Cultural Issues in Oral History.* Logan: Utah State University Press, 2002.

Scott, James C. *The Art of Not Being Governed: An Anarchist History of Upland Southeast Asia.* New Haven, CT: Yale University Press, 2009.

Starr, Louis. "Oral History." In *Oral History: An Interdisciplinary Anthology,* edited by David Dunaway and Willa Baum, 3–26. Nashville, TN: American Association for State and Local History, 1984.

Tapp, Nicholas. *Sovereignty and Rebellion: The White Hmong of Northern Thailand.* New York: Oxford University Press, 1989

Thompson, Paul. "History and the Community," In *Oral History: An Interdisciplinary Anthology,* edited by David Dunaway and Willa Baum, 37–50. Nashville, TN: American Association for State and Local History, 1984.

Thomson, Alistair. "Making the Most of Memories: The Empirical and Subjective Value of Oral Histories." *Transactions of the Royal Historical Society* 9 (January 1999): 291–301.

Vang, Chia Youyee. *Fly until You Die: An Oral History of Hmong Pilots in the Vietnam War.* New York: Oxford University Press, 2019.

Winter, Jay. *Remembering War: The Great War between Historical Memory and History in the Twentieth Century.* New Haven, CT: Yale University Press, 2006.

Wu, Ellen. *The Color of Success: Asian Americans and the Origin of the Model Minority.* Princeton, NJ: Princeton University Press, 2013.

Index

Page numbers in italics refer to illustrations.

Aderholt, Harry, 4
Air America, 5, 39
aircraft: helicopter, 17–19, 23,
  32, 42, 53; B-52, 68; C-47
  (Dakota), 42; Cessna, 42; Piper
  Cub, 42; T-28, 2, 5, 15–18,
  23, 39–42, *44, 47*, 53, 59–60,
  62–64, 66, 68, *136*

Baez, Joan, 105–*106*

California, 125, 128, 130;
  Sacramento, 129
Central Intelligence Agency
  (CIA), 1, 4–6, 17–18, 30, 37,
  39–40, 52, 103, 105, 109
Cha, Sua, 27
Chao Pha Khao, 5, 15, 23
Chong, Youa, 89–94
communist, 3–4, 16–19, 70, 72,
  82, 88

Daniels, Jerry, 105, 109

First Indochina War, 4, 27
France 4–5, 28, 34, 40;
  colonialism, 3–4, 28, 34

Georgia, 119, 125, 129–131;
  Atlanta, 122, 126; Chamblee,
  122

Her, Xai, 51–52
Her, Yee, 31–32
Hmong: Chao Fa resistance
  fighters, 88–89, 91–92;
  diaspora, 6–7, 67; history, 2,
  28; New Year, 52, 86; pilots,
  1–2, 15, 20–21, 23, 39–45, 49,
  59–64, 81–82, 104, 134, 136,
  141n2; polygamy, 19, 27, 31,
  36, 84, 87, 102, 109; spiritual
  practices, 20, 22, 64–65, 69,
  71, 79, 97, 101–102

International office of Migration,
  113

INDEX

Kmhmu, 41, 68, 70, 92, 141n1–142n2

Lai, Kou (Niam Kub Laij), 78–80, 82–86
Lair, James William "Bill," 4
Lao Laum Phao (United Lao Race), 36
Laos: Aviation Laotiénne (Lao Aviation), 4; Ban Khu, 81–82, 87–88, 90; Dong Dok, 34, 36, 40; Khang Khay, 29, 31, 72, 86; Lao People's Democratic Republic, 72; Military Region II, 4–5, 18, 40, 60; Phone Kheng, 41; Phonsavan, 73, 76–78, 81–82, 86, 141n1; Plain of Jars, 68, 141n1; Royal Lao Air Force, 4, 40; Royal Lao Army (RLA), 3–4, 39; Royal Lao Government, 3; Sam Thong, 39; Savannakhet, 41; Vientiane, 17, 19, 31–33, 35–36, 40, 52, 60–61; Xiengkhouang province, 30–31, 67
Lee, Lue, 40, 104
Lee, Nao Yeng, 30
Lee, Ying, 41
Lo, Ge, 41
Lo, Neng, 40
Long Cheng, 17, 19, 30–32, 34, 36, 39, 42, 49–53, 55, 59–62, 72–73, 76, 78, 81, 91, 98, 103

Mekong River, 92–94, 103, 134
Military Assistance and Advisory Group (MAAG), 3
Minnesota, 118, 125–126, 128, 131; St. Paul, 128
Mobile Training Teams (MTTs), 4
Moua, Ber (Muas Npawv), 81–83, 85–86
Moua, Chai Yang (Caiv Yaj Muas), 111

Moua, Chue, 24
Moua, Gao, 37
Moua, Ong, 10, 19–25, 49–56, 64, 79–81, 89, 97, 130–131

Nixon, Richard, 68
nongovernmental organizations (NGOs), 103

Operation Linebacker, 68
Operation Momentum, 4

Pao, Father Nhia (Txiv plig Nyiaj Pov), 35
Pao, Vang, 4, 17–19, 37, 40, 42, 59, 72, 75, 89, 91, 105, 109
Paris Peace Accord, 71
Pathet Lao, 3, 18, 69
Pennsylvania, 111, 113, 114, 116; Freeport, 117; Reading 116–117
Phouma, Prince Souvanna, 3
prison camp, 72: Nam Kien, 67– 68, 76, 82–83, 86, 104, 137
prisoner of war (POW), 1–2, 12–13, 66–72, 75, 79, 83, 89, 97, 99, 141n1

refugee camps, 6, 13, 83, 91, 102, 105, 107, 110, 112, 130; Ban Vinai, 89, 100, 102–106, 111; Nong Khai, 95, 97–103, 142n1

Sayavong, John Bounchanh, 16–18, 136, 141n1

Thailand, 2–4, 39–41, 44, 55, 63, 83, 89, 91, 93, 100, 105, 127–128; Bangkok, 111–113; Thai Police Aerial Reinforcement Units (PARU), 4; Udorn, 40, 43, 60; Udorn Royal Thai Air Force Base, 5, 46
Thao, Yee (Nyaj Yig Thoj), 68

INDEX

United Nations Border Relief Operation (UNBRO), 103
United Nations High Commissioner for Refugees (UNHCR), 105
U.S. Air Force (USAF), 1–2, 6, *47*
U.S. Operations Mission (USOM), 3
U.S. Secret War, 1, 3, 9, 30

Vang, Bee, 24, 89, 91
Vang, Neng, 105
Vang, Seng, 22–23
Vang, Sue, 60
Vang, Toua, 40
Vientiane Agreement, 71
Vietminh, 4
Vietnam, 2–4, 16, 20–21, 68, 71; Saigon, 17
Vietnam War, 1–2, 6–8, 20, 30, 68, 124, 133

Water Pump Program, 1, 5–6, 139n1
Wisconsin: Appleton, 118, 126–127; Milwaukee, 119, *121*; Sheboygan, 118–119, *136*

Xaho (Xaj Hob), 27, 29, 54
Xiong, Kee, 71
Xiong, Koua, 16–17, 44, *136*
Xiong, Ly Tou, 104
Xiong, Yang, 60

Yang, Chai Moua (Caiv Muas Yaj), 27, 111, 113–116
Yang, Chia (Yaj Txiab), 116
Yang, Ena (Sinxai Moua), 10, 85, 87–94, 98–99, 105, 110–119, 122–129, 131
Yang, Pheng, 19–21, 50, 55–*56*, 79–80, 100–101, 109, *111*–113, *123*, 125–127, 130–131
Yang, Sai Shoua (Xaiv Suav Yaj), 91
Yang, Shoua, 37
Yang, Ta, 110–*114*, *123*, 125
Yang, Tong Kai (Tooj Kaim Yaj), 86, 88, 90
Yang, Va Chao (Vam Choj Yaj), 89
Yang, Xia Sher (Txhaij Sawm Yaj), 102, 118
Yang, Youa Chong (Ntsuab Txoov Yaj), 49–*50*, 53
Yang, Youa Tong, 29, 31–32

Chia Youyee Vang is Professor of History at the University of Wisconsin–Milwaukee. She is the author of *Fly Until You Die: An Oral History of Hmong Pilots in the Vietnam War* and *Hmong America: Reconstructing Community in Diaspora*, and the coeditor of *Claiming Place: On the Agency of Hmong Women*.

Also in the series *Asian American History and Culture*

Audrey Wu Clark, *The Asian American Avant-Garde: Universalist Aspirations in Modernist Literature and Art*

Eric Tang, *Unsettled: Cambodian Refugees in the New York City Hyperghetto*

Jeffrey Santa Ana, *Racial Feelings: Asian America in a Capitalist Culture of Emotion*

Jiemin Bao, *Creating a Buddhist Community: A Thai Temple in Silicon Valley*

Elda E. Tsou, *Unquiet Tropes: Form, Race, and Asian American Literature*

Tarry Hum, *Making a Global Immigrant Neighborhood: Brooklyn's Sunset Park*

Ruth Mayer, *Serial Fu Manchu: The Chinese Supervillain and the Spread of Yellow Peril Ideology*

Karen Kuo, *East Is West and West Is East: Gender, Culture, and Interwar Encounters between Asia and America*

Kieu-Linh Caroline Valverde, *Transnationalizing Viet Nam: Community, Culture, and Politics in the Diaspora*

Lan P. Duong, *Treacherous Subjects: Gender, Culture, and Trans-Vietnamese Feminism*

Kristi Brian, *Reframing Transracial Adoption: Adopted Koreans, White Parents, and the Politics of Kinship*

Belinda Kong, *Tiananmen Fictions outside the Square: The Chinese Literary Diaspora and the Politics of Global Culture*

Bindi V. Shah, *Laotian Daughters: Working toward Community, Belonging, and Environmental Justice*

Cherstin M. Lyon, *Prisons and Patriots: Japanese American Wartime Citizenship, Civil Disobedience, and Historical Memory*

Shelley Sang-Hee Lee, *Claiming the Oriental Gateway: Prewar Seattle and Japanese America*

Isabelle Thuy Pelaud, *This Is All I Choose to Tell: History and Hybridity in Vietnamese American Literature*

Christian Collet and Pei-te Lien, eds., *The Transnational Politics of Asian Americans*

Min Zhou, *Contemporary Chinese America: Immigration, Ethnicity, and Community Transformation*

Kathleen S. Yep, *Outside the Paint: When Basketball Ruled at the Chinese Playground*

Benito M. Vergara Jr., *Pinoy Capital: The Filipino Nation in Daly City*

Jonathan Y. Okamura, *Ethnicity and Inequality in Hawai'i*

Sucheng Chan and Madeline Y. Hsu, eds., *Chinese Americans and the Politics of Race and Culture*

K. Scott Wong, *Americans First: Chinese Americans and the Second World War*

Lisa Yun, *The Coolie Speaks: Chinese Indentured Laborers and African Slaves in Cuba*

Estella Habal, *San Francisco's International Hotel: Mobilizing the Filipino American Community in the Anti-eviction Movement*

Thomas P. Kim, *The Racial Logic of Politics: Asian Americans and Party Competition*

Sucheng Chan, ed., *The Vietnamese American 1.5 Generation: Stories of War, Revolution, Flight, and New Beginnings*

Antonio T. Tiongson Jr., Edgardo V. Gutierrez, and Ricardo V. Gutierrez, eds., *Positively No Filipinos Allowed: Building Communities and Discourse*

Sucheng Chan, ed., *Chinese American Transnationalism: The Flow of People, Resources, and Ideas between China and America during the Exclusion Era*

Rajini Srikanth, *The World Next Door: South Asian American Literature and the Idea of America*

Keith Lawrence and Floyd Cheung, eds., *Recovered Legacies: Authority and Identity in Early Asian American Literature*

Linda Trinh Võ, *Mobilizing an Asian American Community*

Franklin S. Odo, *No Sword to Bury: Japanese Americans in Hawai'i during World War II*

Josephine Lee, Imogene L. Lim, and Yuko Matsukawa, eds., *Re/collecting Early Asian America: Essays in Cultural History*

Linda Trinh Võ and Rick Bonus, eds., *Contemporary Asian American Communities: Intersections and Divergences*

Sunaina Marr Maira, *Desis in the House: Indian American Youth Culture in New York City*

Teresa Williams-León and Cynthia Nakashima, eds., *The Sum of Our Parts: Mixed-Heritage Asian Americans*

Tung Pok Chin with Winifred C. Chin, *Paper Son: One Man's Story*

Amy Ling, ed., *Yellow Light: The Flowering of Asian American Arts*

Rick Bonus, *Locating Filipino Americans: Ethnicity and the Cultural Politics of Space*

Darrell Y. Hamamoto and Sandra Liu, eds., *Countervisions: Asian American Film Criticism*

Martin F. Manalansan IV, ed., *Cultural Compass: Ethnographic Explorations of Asian America*

Ko-lin Chin, *Smuggled Chinese: Clandestine Immigration to the United States*

Evelyn Hu-DeHart, ed., *Across the Pacific: Asian Americans and Globalization*

Soo-Young Chin, *Doing What Had to Be Done: The Life Narrative of Dora Yum Kim*

Robert G. Lee, *Orientals: Asian Americans in Popular Culture*

David L. Eng and Alice Y. Hom, eds., *Q & A: Queer in Asian America*

K. Scott Wong and Sucheng Chan, eds., *Claiming America: Constructing Chinese American Identities during the Exclusion Era*

Lavina Dhingra Shankar and Rajini Srikanth, eds., *A Part, Yet Apart: South Asians in Asian America*

Jere Takahashi, *Nisei/Sansei: Shifting Japanese American Identities and Politics*

Velina Hasu Houston, ed., *But Still, Like Air, I'll Rise: New Asian American Plays*

Josephine Lee, *Performing Asian America: Race and Ethnicity on the Contemporary Stage*

Deepika Bahri and Mary Vasudeva, eds., *Between the Lines: South Asians and Postcoloniality*

E. San Juan Jr., *The Philippine Temptation: Dialectics of Philippines–U.S. Literary Relations*

Carlos Bulosan and E. San Juan Jr., eds., *The Cry and the Dedication*

Carlos Bulosan and E. San Juan Jr., eds., *On Becoming Filipino: Selected Writings of Carlos Bulosan*

Vicente L. Rafael, ed., *Discrepant Histories: Translocal Essays on Filipino Cultures*

Yen Le Espiritu, *Filipino American Lives*

Paul Ong, Edna Bonacich, and Lucie Cheng, eds., *The New Asian Immigration in Los Angeles and Global Restructuring*

Chris Friday, *Organizing Asian American Labor: The Pacific Coast Canned-Salmon Industry, 1870–1942*

Sucheng Chan, ed., *Hmong Means Free: Life in Laos and America*

Timothy P. Fong, *The First Suburban Chinatown: The Remaking of Monterey Park, California*

William Wei, *The Asian American Movement*

Yen Le Espiritu, *Asian American Panethnicity*

Velina Hasu Houston, ed., *The Politics of Life*

Renqiu Yu, *To Save China, To Save Ourselves: The Chinese Hand Laundry Alliance of New York*

Shirley Geok-lin Lim and Amy Ling, eds., *Reading the Literatures of Asian America*

Karen Isaksen Leonard, *Making Ethnic Choices: California's Punjabi Mexican Americans*

Gary Y. Okihiro, *Cane Fires: The Anti-Japanese Movement in Hawaii, 1865–1945*

Sucheng Chan, *Entry Denied: Exclusion and the Chinese Community in America, 1882–1943*